A Grab for the Orinoco: America and Venezuela's Oil Reconquest

Subtitle: *Issues, Strategies and Consequences of the Return of Energy Giants After the Fall of Maduro.*

Work written by:
Nachida HAROUNI

First publication
Draft2digital
January 2026

AUTHOR'S NOTE

This book, *"Main Basse sur l'Orénoque" (Hands Off the Orinoco)* , is intended as a warning. It is not science fiction, but **"Design Fiction"** : a realistic projection based on current vulnerabilities (US refining, Chinese debt, the fragility of the dollar).

WARNING TO THE READER

This book is a work of **speculative fiction** (*Design Fiction*). Although the story takes place in a realistic geographical and economic setting, and mentions real public figures, existing businesses, and technologies for the sake of narrative realism, the events, dialogues, and situations described (including the 2026 invasion, specific contracts, and acts of corruption) are products of the author's imagination. They should not be interpreted as established facts or official predictions.

Table of Contents:

CHAPTER 1: The Missing Link in American Refining

- *The obsession with API density and why Texas was no longer sufficient.*

CHAPTER 2: The "Houston Plan"

- *The logistical invasion and the rewriting of oil laws.*

CHAPTER 3: Disguised Privatization

- *The purge of managers, the end of the welfare state, and social apartheid.*

CHAPTER 4: The Debt War and the Dragon's Counterattack

- *How China has transformed international law into a weapon of war.*

CHAPTER 5: The Texas Dilemma

- *The revolt of shale producers and energy blackmail against Europe.*

CHAPTER 6: The Vultures of the Construction Industry

- *The economics of reconstruction, corruption and the unintentional financing of crime.*

CHAPTER 7: The Hybrid Insurrection

- *Drones, sabotage and the unnatural alliance between gangs and the military.*

CHAPTER 8 (CONCLUSION): The Crash of Truth

- *The financial collapse, the American withdrawal, and the new world order.*

INTRODUCTION: NOISE AND THE BILL

Caracas, January 19, 2026.

The dust has barely settled on the ruins of the Fuerte Tiuna complex. Less than three weeks ago, on the night of January 2nd to 3rd, the world watched in stunned disbelief as the flashes of American precision strikes illuminated the Caracas sky. Operation *"Absolute Resolve"* was sold to the international media by the White House as an act of surgical justice: the neutralization of a regime labeled narco-terrorist and the spectacular exfiltration of the former president to a federal cell in New York.

On the 24-hour news channels, they still talk about "freedom," "democratic transition," and "the end of tyranny." Images of jubilant or angry crowds are playing on a loop. But in the glass towers of Houston, at the headquarters of **Titan Energy** , and in the hushed offices of **Botts Legal** , the sound of missiles has already given way to the studious silence of Excel spreadsheets and geological maps.

For the informed expert, the military operation was not an end in itself. It was an **operation to unlock the situation** .

This book doesn't tell the official story of the 2026 war. It doesn't dwell on the legal fate of the ousted leaders, nor on the political upheavals of the transitional government. This book tells the true story unfolding now, far from the cameras: that of the largest energy asset transfer of the 21st century, orchestrated by an unprecedented alliance between the Pentagon and Wall Street.

The Paradox of American Power

Why would the United States, the world's leading oil producer thanks to the shale *oil revolution* , take the political and military risk of direct intervention in Venezuela? The answer lies not in international law books, but in hydrocarbon chemistry.

America suffers from a major industrial paradox. It produces oil that is too light, too "soft." Yet the vast refining infrastructure of the Gulf of Mexico—the coast of Texas and Louisiana—was designed to process heavy, viscous, sulfur-laden crude. For years, giants like **Alamo Refining** and **Spartan Downstream** have been bleeding dry. They are forced to import at exorbitant prices or blend unsuitable crudes, eroding their profit margins.

The Orinoco Belt, with its 300 billion barrels of proven reserves of extra-heavy crude oil, is not just a Venezuelan asset. It is, geologically and industrially, the missing piece of the American energy puzzle.

From Geopolitics to Geo-economics

The military intervention has removed the political obstacle. The path is now clear for the return of the American *supermajors* . But make no mistake: this is not a return to normalcy. It is a complete overhaul.

PetroVen , the national company once the pride of socialism, is a smoldering ruin. It no longer has the capital or the technology. Venezuela is a country rich in mineral resources, but bankrupt on the surface.

Therefore, the equation facing us at the beginning of 2026 is stark: to rebuild the country, sovereignty must be ceded. We are entering the era of **privatization out of necessity** .

The Stakes of this Work

In the following pages, we will dissect the mechanics of this reconquest.

- We will analyze how Washington used international law to erase Venezuela's debt to China (**SinoOil**), transforming a financial dispute into a weapon of war.
- We will reveal the behind-the-scenes story of the reconstruction, where billions of dollars disappear into the pockets of intermediaries like **Bauchet Construction** , ultimately inadvertently funding the criminal gangs they were supposed to be fighting.
- Finally, we will explore the hidden cost of this war: the revolt of independent producers in Texas, sacrificed on the altar of

refiner profitability, and the energy blackmail imposed on Europe.

The attack on January 3rd lasted a few hours. The economic battle for control of the Orinoco River, however, is only just beginning. And the outcome of this battle will determine not only the price of your gasoline, but the balance of power in the world for the next twenty years.

Welcome to the reality of *raw materials* .

CHAPTER 1: THE MISSING LINK IN AMERICAN REFINING

Or why America is dying of thirst in the middle of an ocean of oil.

To understand why Delta Force soldiers landed in Caracas on the night of January 3, 2026, one shouldn't look at DEA drug trafficking reports or fiery speeches about democracy delivered at the UN. Instead, one should look at a geological map of the Permian Basin in Texas and overlay it with the engineering plans of the refineries along the Gulf *Coast* .

There is a persistent myth, perpetuated by successive Washington administrations since the mid-2010s: that of "Energy Independence." According to this narrative, the fracking revolution *freed* the United States from its dependence on petro-monarchies and unstable dictatorships. It is a convenient political lie, but an industrial aberration.

The reality, which Operation *Absolute Resolve* has just brought to light with unprecedented brutality, is that the United States suffers from a fatal mismatch between what it produces and what it consumes. America is a giant with feet of clay, capable of flooding the world with light oil, but incapable of running its own factories at full capacity without outside help.

This first chapter aims to deconstruct the American paradox. We will delve into the chemistry of hydrocarbons and the financial statements of "Super-Majors" like **Titan Energy** and **AmeriCorp** to demonstrate a simple truth: Venezuelan oil is not a luxury for the United States. It is a matter of national industrial security.

1. The Tyranny of Density API

To the layperson, "oil is oil." A black, viscous substance that transforms into gasoline. For the petrochemical engineer, this statement is heresy that costs billions of dollars. The global crude oil market is governed by a ruthless measurement scale: **API gravity** (American Petroleum Institute gravity).

This is where Uncle Sam's problem lies.

Since 2010, US production has exploded, making the country the world's leading producer. But 90% of this new shale production (Permian Basin, Eagle Ford, Bakken) is light sweet crude , **with** *a* density above 40° API. It is a champagne-colored, very fluid liquid, low in sulfur.

At the opposite end of the geological spectrum are **heavy oil** (below 22° API) and **extra-heavy oil** (below 10° API). This is what Venezuela produces in the Orinoco Belt. At room temperature, it's not a liquid; it's practically bitumen. A black molasses, rich in heavy metals (vanadium, nickel) and sulfur.

The strategic problem is this: oil doesn't go directly into your car's tank. It has to go through a refinery. And American refineries don't want Texas "Champagne." They want Venezuelan "Melasse."

2. PADD 3: A Cathedral of Rust Designed for Heavy Duty

America's energy heart beats in **PADD 3** (*Petroleum Administration for Defense District 3*). This administrative area covers Texas, Louisiana, and Mississippi. It concentrates more than 50% of the total refining capacity of the United States and represents the most sophisticated industrial complex on the planet.

In the 1990s and 2000s, long before anyone imagined extracting shale oil, the industry giants— **Titan Energy** , **AmeriCorp Petroleum** , **Alamo Refining** , and **Spartan Downstream** —made a colossal bet. Forecasts at the time predicted the end of light oil (easy to refine) and the future dominance of heavy, dirty oils (more difficult to extract, but cheaper to buy).

this price difference, American refiners have invested hundreds of billions of dollars to transform their facilities into technological marvels. They have built **coking and deep hydrocracking units. These colossal machines—steel towers as tall as 30-story buildings—are**

designed to take the heaviest, dirtiest , and cheapest crude oil on the market, break down its complex carbon molecules at high temperatures, and extract high-quality gasoline and diesel.

It's a brilliant business model, but it has one rigid flaw: the metallurgy.

A "complex" refinery configured for heavy crude *must* process heavy crude. If you feed a coking unit with light shale oil from Texas, you're underutilizing the plant. Economically, it's comparable to buying an industrial rock crusher to crush strawberries: it works, but it's a terrible waste of capital.

The Economics of the "Crack Spread": The Calculation That Justified the War

To understand why the oil lobbies ultimately supported the 2026 military intervention, you have to get out the calculator and look at the **"Crack Spread"** (the gross refining margin). That's the crux of the matter.

Let's compare the situation of an **Alamo Refining plant** in Louisiana at the end of 2025:

1. **"Independence" scenario (US oil only):**

   The refinery buys a barrel of *WTI Midland* (light Texas) at $75. This oil produces a lot of gasoline, but the market is saturated. The net back margin barely fluctuates between **$8 and $10 per barrel** .

1. **Scenario "Symbiosis" (Venezuelan Oil):**

   The same refinery buys a barrel of *Merey 16* (Venezuelan). Due to its poor quality, this barrel is sold at a massive discount *on* the international market. Purchase price: $55.

Thanks to its *cokers* , the refinery transforms this cheap sludge into diesel and kerosene, products with very high added value. The net margin jumps to **$25 or $30 per barrel** .

The equation is unforgiving. A Gulf refinery deprived of heavy crude loses approximately $15 to $20 in pure profit on *every* barrel processed. Multiply that by the millions of barrels processed daily by **Alamo** or **AmeriCorp** , and you arrive at an annual shortfall in tens of billions of dollars. By 2025, the American refining system was bleeding money, not from a lack of volume, but from a "dietary error."

3. The Perfect Storm: The Collapse of Alternatives (2022-2025)

If the United States had been able to find this heavy oil elsewhere, Operation *Absolute Resolve* might never have happened. But history dictated that all alternative sources dried up simultaneously.

- **The Russian Impasse:** Until 2022, the US compensated for Venezuela's lack of supply with Russian fuel oil (*M-100*). The war in Ukraine and the sanctions against **Volga Oil** (the Russian giant) cut off this supply, creating an immediate vacuum.
- **The Mexican Decline:** Mexico has reduced its exports to supply its own nationalist refinery in Dos Bocas.
- **The Canadian Nightmare:** Alberta's tar sands oil is a perfect substitute, but transporting it to Texas is a logistical nightmare. Without the Keystone XL pipeline, it must travel by rail or on congested pipelines, making it prohibitively expensive.

By the end of 2025, heavy crude oil stocks in PADD 3 had reached a critical level. The CEOs of **Spartan Downstream** and Alamo **Refining** warned the White House: diesel prices in the US were threatening to skyrocket. Only one option remained on the world map: Venezuela, located just four days away by ship.

4. Autopsy of a failure: The strategy of sanctions

Why did the military option become inevitable in January 2026? Because the silent economic war had failed.

Previous administrations had bet on financial strangulation. By cutting off oil purchases in 2019, Washington thought the Maduro regime would collapse within months. This was a miscalculation that underestimated the resilience of the black market.

Instead of stopping, Venezuelan oil went underground.

A " *Dark Fleet* " of old tankers, operating without GPS transponders, began to transport crude to China, often via ship-to-ship transfers off Malaysia to cover their tracks.

The result was catastrophic for American interests:

1. China was buying oil at rock-bottom prices (-40%), strengthening its economy via **SinoOil** .
2. American refiners (**Route 66 Energy** , **AmeriCorp**) were deprived of their vital raw material.
3. Maduro survived thanks to suitcases of cash, impervious to Western banking pressures.

By the end of 2025, the assessment at the White House was bitter: the sanctions were punishing Texas more than Caracas. With the economic engine broken, only the military hammer remained to "reset" the flow of goods and services.

5. The VenUSA Petroleum Case Study: The Hostage Freed

At the heart of this war is a company whose name is familiar to all American motorists, but whose strategic importance is often ignored: **VenUSA Petroleum** (formerly known by its real name Citgo before restructuring).

A wholly owned subsidiary of the Venezuelan national oil company **PetroVen** , **VenUSA** owns three major refineries in the United States

(Lake Charles, Lemont, Corpus Christi). These plants are technological marvels designed specifically to process Venezuelan oil.

During the diplomatic crisis (2019-2025), **VenUSA** found itself held hostage. International creditors (such as the mining company **CrystalGold** and the oil company **Phillips-Conrad**) attempted to seize the company in Delaware courts to recover debts owed by Caracas. The US administration protected **VenUSA** through temporary executive orders, knowing that if the company were dismantled and sold off piecemeal, the United States would lose the only refining capacity capable of processing large quantities of Venezuelan crude oil on the day of the "reopening."

The January 3rd intervention cut the Gordian knot. By installing a new government in Caracas, Washington secured the asset. **VenUSA** will not be sold. It will be the spearhead of reconstruction. It is through its terminals that the crude oil from the Orinoco will once again flow northward. **VenUSA** is the industrial prize that alone justifies the operation.

6. The Voice from Within

To conclude this technical section, let's hear from those who operate behind the scenes of political decision-making. We were able to speak, on condition of anonymity, with a former vice president in charge of supply chain strategy for a Houston-based super-major (likely **Titan Energy** or **AmeriCorp**). The interview took place on January 12, 2026, nine days after the attack.

Q: Were you surprised by the military intervention?

R: Surprised by the date? Maybe. By the action? Not at all. Our models have been running in the red for two years. You have to understand the atmosphere in Houston in 2025. The government was asking us to lower the price of diesel at the pump to curb inflation, but it was forbidding us from buying the only raw material—heavy crude—capable of producing it cheaply. It was political schizophrenia.

Q: Yet we're talking about restoring democracy...

R: (Bitter laughter) Look, I'm not a diplomat, I'm an engineer. If Venezuela's subsoil were full of broccoli, the special forces would have stayed in North Carolina. The reality is that our refineries were starting to cannibalize their profit margins. We were importing Canadian crude by train; it was a logistical absurdity!

Q: And now?

R: Now, we're going to restore order. **PetroVen** is an industrial disaster. There are leaks everywhere. We're going to bring our teams, our capital, our technology via **Burton & Hall** and **Alsace Tech** . We're not going there to play politics, but to reconnect the pipelines. It's a return to the logic of gravity: the heavy oil from the Orinoco must go to the nearest plant capable of processing it, which is us. It's as simple as that.

A. Pascagoula's "Red Alert": When chemistry says stop

AmeriCorp Refinery, Pascagoula, Mississippi. October 14, 2025.

The noise in a refinery is constant, a background hum that becomes invisible to the human ear after a few years. But that morning, the noise changed. It was a high-pitched whine, followed by a deep rumble that rattled the windows of the central control room.

Mike "Iron" Henderson, the refinery's operations manager, dropped his coffee. On the wall of screens, a red alarm was flashing on Coker Unit *2* .

"Cut the power!" he yelled into his microphone. "Cut everything off, damn it!"

The incident lasted four minutes. A safety valve burst, releasing a cloud of toxic vapor into the atmosphere. There were no fatalities, only two workers suffering from smoke inhalation. But for Henderson, it was a harbinger of disaster.

An hour later, sitting in his office with the chemical engineers, he was looking at the analysis reports for the crude oil they had fed into the machine. "Take a look at this, Mike," said the chief chemist, throwing the file on the table. "This is shale crude from the Eagle Ford Basin. API gravity of 46°. It's water."

“We had no choice,” Henderson replied. “Canadian heavy crude stocks are empty. The Alberta train derailed last week. We had to supplement with light crude.”

"The coking ovens can't handle it, Mike. They're designed to burn heavy, dirty stuff. If you give them light stuff, the temperature rises too quickly. The metal walls become brittle. This morning, we almost blew a hole in the tank. Next time, it'll really explode and we'll level half the Mississippi River."

Henderson picked up his phone. He wasn't going to call maintenance. He was going to call headquarters in San Ramon.

"Get me the VP of Procurement. Tell him this is an industrial emergency. Tell him that if I don't get heavy crude, real heavy crude, within three weeks, I'm shutting down the refinery. I'm not going to blow up my plant because Washington is messing around with sanctions. I need Venezuelan crude, and I need it now."

This phone call, repeated by the plant managers of **Alamo Refining** in Texas and **Spartan Downstream** in Louisiana, was the first domino to fall. The American industrial base had just signaled that it was dying from oil "malnutrition."

B. The "River Oaks" Dinner: The Coalition of Rivals

River Oaks Country Club, Houston, TX. November 2, 2025.

It's the most exclusive place in Texas. The talk is golf, hunting, and billions. That evening, in a private room with mahogany paneling, an unlikely encounter took place.

Around the table sat three men who, under normal circumstances, would spend their time trying to destroy each other on the stock markets:

1. The CEO of **Titan Energy** (the largest American oil company).
2. The CEO of **AmeriCorp Petroleum** .
3. The CEO of **Alamo Refining** (the largest independent refiner).

They hadn't touched their *Ribeye steaks* . The atmosphere was somber.

The head of **Alamo** spoke first. He was a stocky man, known for his outspokenness.

"My refining margins are at $4 a barrel. At this rate, I'll default on my bond debt in February. My plants are running at 70% capacity because I can't find any more heavy crude. The Russians are under embargo, the Mexicans are keeping everything for themselves. That leaves only Canada, and their pipelines are bursting at the seams. We're suffocating."

The CEO of **Titan Energy** , a cold man with rimless glasses, nodded.

“It’s no better for us. Our shale wells in the Permian are producing at full capacity, but nobody in the US wants our light crude because your refineries can’t process it. We’re forced to export it at rock-bottom prices to Asia. It’s absurd. We sell our good oil to China for a pittance, and we have nothing to run our own plants.”

The head of **AmeriCorp** placed a map on the table. It was a map of the Caribbean Sea. He put his finger on the coast of Venezuela.

— There are 300 billion barrels here. It's *Merey 16 crude* . Exactly what you need to save your mills, Alamo. And exactly what you need to blend with our shale, Titan.

"It's under sanctions," the Alamo boss reminded everyone. "And Maduro sold all of that to the Chinese company **SinoOil** ."

“Maduro is a solvable problem,” the Titan boss said calmly. “The real problem is Washington. They’re afraid of public opinion. They’re afraid of the ‘war for oil’ image.”

“If we do nothing,” said the head of AmeriCorp, “the price of diesel will rise to $7 a gallon next March. The American economy will enter a recession. And we will lose our global supremacy to Indian and Chinese refineries that buy Venezuelan oil on the black market.”

A silence fell. They all knew what it meant. This wasn't just ordinary lobbying anymore. This was about demanding regime change.

"How much does it cost to get **PetroVen** up and running again?" Titan asked.

"50 billion over five years," AmeriCorp replied. "But if we control the country, we'll get paid off the land. We'll use the Iraqi model, but improved. We'll secure the assets, kick out the Chinese, and connect our pipelines."

— And what about the White House?

— They're being sold the angle of "National Security" and "Fighting China." We're not talking about profit. We're talking about saving America from communist influence. The President will love that.

They raised their glasses of Bourbon. That night, the "Houston Coalition" was born. They would finance, plan, and sell the war.

C. The White Note: The Argument of Fear

Office of the National Security Advisor, Washington DC. November 20, 2025.

The document had no header, no signature. Just a title: *"PROJECTION: BLACKOUT SCENARIO 2026"*.

It had been hand-delivered by a lobbyist from **Botts Legal** (the energy law firm).

The National Security Advisor read it with growing concern.

The memo wasn't about money. It was about survival.

He described a catastrophic scenario for the summer of 2026:

1. Refineries in the Gulf of Mexico are breaking down one after another due to a lack of heavy crude oil.
2. National diesel shortage. Trucks are stopping. Supermarkets are no longer receiving deliveries.
3. Panic on Wall Street. Double-digit inflation.
4. Meanwhile, China (**SinoOil**) takes total control of Venezuela, sets up a naval base in Puerto Cabello and points missiles towards Florida.

The memo concluded with a terse sentence: *"Inaction leads to the loss of the Western Hemisphere. Reopening Venezuela under American supervision is not an economic option, it is an imperative of national survival."*

The Councillor looked up at his deputy.

— Is that credible?

— Our energy analysts say they're right about the refining situation. We're on a knife-edge. If just one big refinery breaks down this winter, we'll have food riots.

— And what about the military option?

"The Pentagon has had a plan ready since 2019. Operation *Absolute Resolve* . They say they can take Caracas in 48 hours. The real problem is what comes after.

" "We don't care about what comes after," the Advisor retorted. "If gas prices are $6 in November for the elections, we're finished. Prepare a briefing for the President. Tell him Maduro is about to give the Chinese a nuclear base. That'll motivate him."

Thus, the war was sold not on the basis of truth (the need for heavy crude oil), but on a geopolitical lie (the imminent Chinese threat). The machinery of the deep state was aligned with Houston's interests.

D. The "Caribbean Star" Affair: The Manufactured Casus Belli

Caribbean Sea, International Waters. December 24, 2025.

A trigger was needed. A spark to justify the intervention in the eyes of the world.

The *Caribbean Star* was an old tanker flying the Liberian flag, secretly chartered by a CIA front company, but officially carrying humanitarian gas.

It was deliberately sailing close to the edge of Venezuelan territorial waters.

At 2:00 a.m., a Venezuelan Navy speedboat approached. The Venezuelans' orders were clear: intercept the smugglers.

The captain of the *Caribbean Star* sent a distress message: *"Mayday, Mayday, we are under attack by hostile forces in international waters. They are firing on the crew."*

In reality, the Venezuelans had fired warning shots into the air. But in the grainy video that was looped on **WNN** (World News Network) the following morning, tracers could be seen in the night sky and screams of panic (played by agents) could be heard.

The image of a "humanitarian ship" attacked by Maduro's "brutal regime" went around the world.

At the White House, the President slammed his fist on the table. "This is piracy! They're attacking our ships! This is an act of war!"

No one questioned the ship's actual cargo or its provocative course. Public opinion was inflamed. The CEOs of **Titan** and **AmeriCorp** could breathe a sigh of relief. The war machine was in motion. The technical problem of oil viscosity would be solved by the Tomahawks.

E. The Last Night of Venus (Citgo)

VenUSA Petroleum Headquarters, Houston. January 2, 2026 (Eve of the invasion).

Carlos, the finance director of **VenUSA** (PDVSA's American subsidiary), was looking at his boxes. He had just been "placed on administrative leave" by the American authorities who had taken de facto control of the company.

His replacement, an American court-appointed administrator, entered the office.

— Don't take it personally, Carlos. It's business.

"Business?" Carlos replied in Spanish. "You're stealing from the company. These refineries belong to the Venezuelan people." "They belong to those who can run them," the American retorted. "You have no more oil, Carlos. Your plants are shut down. Tomorrow, everything changes. Tomorrow, the U.S. Navy will reopen the road. In a week, this office will be filled with *Merey crude* . And **VenUSA** will be saved."

— Saved? You're going to turn it into a colony.

"A subsidiary," the American corrected with a cold smile. "A successful subsidiary. Now go home. Watch TV tonight. It'll be quite a show."

Carlos left the glass building. Outside, the air was heavy. He knew that in a few hours, bombs would fall on his homeland. Not to liberate it, but to fill the empty tanks of the refinery he had just left. He understood then, with terrifying clarity, that his country was no longer a nation, but a depreciated asset on the balance sheet of a multinational corporation, ready to be liquidated and restructured.

Conclusion

In January 2026, as American flags discreetly fly over the loading terminals of Puerto José, it must be understood that this war is not a classic territorial conquest.

The United States did not invade Venezuela to steal its oil and resell it on the markets. They invaded Venezuela to **mix** that oil with their own.

It's a forced marriage to save the profitability of the American industrial complex. Texas light crude desperately needed Orinoco heavy crude to add value. Operation *Absolute Resolve* solved the supply problem. But it opened a Pandora's box: now that access is secured militarily, it must be secured industrially. Because the oil is there, underground, but the tool to extract it— **PetroVen** —exists only on paper.

The military phase is over. The colonial engineering phase begins. And as we will see in the next chapter, the reconstruction of the Venezuelan oil industry looks suspiciously like a privatization in all but name, orchestrated by the giants **AmeriCorp** and **Titan Energy** .

CHAPTER 2: THE "HOUSTON PLAN"

Autopsy of an industrial corpse and logistics of resurrection.

Maiquetía International Airport, Venezuela. January 16, 2026.

The civilian area of the airport is still officially closed to commercial traffic. The departure halls are patrolled by units of the US Military Police and a few detachments of the Brazilian army, who have come to provide logistical support. But on the tarmac of the private area, far from the eyes of the **WNN** (World News Network) cameras filming the distribution of humanitarian rations in downtown Caracas, an aerial ballet of a completely different nature has begun.

For the past 72 hours, it's no longer gray C-17 Globemaster cargo planes that are landing. Instead, it's Gulfstream G650 business jets and Bombardier Global Express aircraft, with immaculate white fuselages. They display no national flags, only discreet civilian registrations, often registered in Delaware or Bermuda.

These aircraft do not carry diplomats or aid workers. They carry men in Oxford shirts, without ties, wearing ballistic vests concealed beneath lightweight technical jackets. They carry reinforced briefcases and satellite phones. They are escorted from the bridge by private *contractors* —former British Navy SEALs or SAS paid $1,500 a day.

These men are the vanguard. They are the "Rapid Assessment Teams" *dispatched* by **AmeriCorp Petroleum** , **Titan Energy** , **Burton & Hall** , **Alsace Tech** and **Hughes Drilling** .

If the Pentagon generals led the first week of January, these men are leading the rest of the century. They have on their secure servers a document that no one in Caracas has yet read, but which will govern the lives of 30 million people: the **"Plan for the Stabilization of Venezuelan Hydrocarbons"** , more prosaically nicknamed in the field: the **Houston Protocol** .

This chapter details the implementation of this plan. It recounts how, as the fighting had barely ceased, the largest industrial renovation operation in modern history began. It wasn't about repairing a company. It was about exhuming a corpse, putting it on life support, and forcing it to run a marathon.

1. PetroVen: Anatomy of a Ruin (The "Patient Zero" Report)

To understand the magnitude of the task facing American engineers, one must first accept the reality of what the national company, now referred to in US reports as **PetroVen** (formerly PDVSA), has become.

In the 1990s, the national company was considered the "Saudi Aramco" of Latin America: a state-owned enterprise managed like a private multinational, efficient, technocratic, and respected.

In January 2026, **PetroVen** is no longer an oil company. It is a fictitious employment agency combined with a money laundering machine, sitting on a pile of rusty scrap metal.

AmeriCorp teams (the only Western company to have maintained a minimal presence on site during the crisis years), are terrifying. They describe a level of disrepair that defies industrial comprehension.

Death Lake (Maracaibo Basin)

The Zulia region, the historical cradle of Venezuelan oil, presents a scene of post-apocalyptic desolation. Lake Maracaibo, once the jewel of production, has become a dead zone.

- **Submerged infrastructure:** Of the 15,000 wells drilled in the lake, less than 2,000 were still vaguely active at the end of 2025. The others were abandoned without adequate sealing.
- **The state of the pipelines:** The underwater pipeline network, which runs like a vein along the bottom of the lake, is riddled with leaks. It is estimated that 500 to 1,000 barrels of crude oil have been leaking into the water every day for the past ten years. The water is green, choked by *duckweed* (lemna) fed by

sewage discharges, and black with oil at the surface.

- **Industrial cannibalism:** The gas compression stations, vital for maintaining well pressure, were looted. Copper cables, alloy valves, electric motors: anything of value was dismantled by starving employees or criminal gangs to be sold for scrap in neighboring Colombia.

The Orinoco Belt: The Paralyzed Giant

Further south, in the Faja (the Belt), the situation is different but just as critical. Here, the oil is extra heavy. It needs to be heated and diluted to move.

- **The shortage of diluents:** To transport this "bitumen," **PetroVen** needed to import naphtha or condensate. Due to a lack of cash, imports ceased . As a result, the oil solidified in the pipelines. Hundreds of kilometers of pipes are now blocked by hardened oil, transformed into solid asphalt within the infrastructure itself. These pipelines are beyond repair; they are doomed. New ones will have to be built.
- **The "Upgraders" at a standstill: Jose's** pre-refining plants (*Mejoradores*), designed to convert extra-heavy crude into exportable crude, were operating at only 15% of their capacity. Due to a lack of maintenance, the distillation towers are corroded and the heat exchangers are leaking. Industrial fires there had become a weekly occurrence in 2024 and 2025.

Human Hemorrhage

But the most irreversible damage isn't material. It's "Human Capital."

By 2026, the remaining "engineers" at **PetroVen** are often inexperienced young people, paid $20 a month, who survive by stealing equipment. There are no more senior geologists, no more fluid specialists, no more master drillers. The company's institutional memory has been erased.

It is on this field of ruins that the Americans land. They are not there to "collaborate" with **PetroVen** . They are there to replace it, pure and simple.

2. The Genesis of the "Houston Protocol": Preparing for the Invasion

Unlike the 2003 invasion of Iraq, where the Bush administration was notable for its lack of post-conflict planning ("Day After"), Operation *Absolute Resolve* was prepared with Swiss watchmaker-like precision by the private sector.

History will remember that the fate of Venezuela was not decided at the White House, but at the **Petroleum Club in Houston** , on the top floor of the **Titan Energy building** .

By mid-2024, an informal working group had been formed. It included:

1. **The "Major" teams: AmeriCorp** (which led the consortium), **Titan Energy** , and **Phillips-Conrad** .
2. **The "Services": Burton & Hall** and **Alsace Tech** , who provide the technology and the arms.
3. **The "Banks":** Representatives from **Manhattan Chase Bank and** *private equity* funds specializing in distressed energy such as **Hades Capital** .
4. **The Shadow of the State:** An Assistant Under Secretary of the US Department of Energy, present as an "observer".

The philosophy of the plan

Their conclusion was simple: the regime was going to fall. When that happened, a complete legal and security vacuum would ensue. If American companies didn't come up with a "turnkey" plan within 48 hours, China or chaos would prevail.

The **Houston Protocol** rests on three brutal pillars:

Pillar A: The Operational Free Zone

The plan involves dividing oil-producing areas into "Energy Security Districts." Within these districts, normal Venezuelan law no longer applies. Customs is handled by private companies like **Global Express** (DHL) to expedite the import of goods. Security is provided by private military companies (PMCs) such as **Sentinel Global** , not by the local police. Payments are made exclusively in US dollars.

Pillar B: Priority "Cost Recovery"

American companies will advance the money for reconstruction (CAPEX). But they will be reimbursed *before* a single cent reaches the Venezuelan state coffers.

The mechanism is called **Accelerated Cost Reimbursement** . On each barrel extracted:

- The first 40% covers operational costs (OPEX).
- The next 40% reimburses the initial investment.
- The remaining 20% is shared between the operator and the state.

  This means that for the first 5 to 7 years, Venezuela will receive virtually no significant oil revenue. Everything will be used to pay for its own "liberation."

Pillar C: The administrative purge

PetroVen 's current workforce and the reinstatement of a pre-established list of 5,000 Venezuelan engineers from the diaspora, currently based in Houston, Miami or Calgary.

3. Phase 1: The Logistics Shock (The first 90 days)

Return to January 19, 2026.

The plan is being unveiled. The first step is not to drill. It is to restore basic industrial civilization.

The logistics put in place are comparable to the Normandy landings, but with pipelines instead of tanks.

Electrical Emergency

You can't pump oil without electricity. But Venezuela's electrical grid is unstable.

Burton & Hall 's solution ? Not to connect to the national grid.

Giant barges are en route from Florida and Texas, transporting **modular power plants** and mobile gas turbines. These units will be installed directly on the oil fields.

The goal: To make the oil fields energy self-sufficient. It doesn't matter if Caracas is plunged into darkness; the pumps in the Orinoco Belt must run 24/7.

Securing the Terminals (José and Puerto La Cruz)

Export terminals are the bottlenecks. That's where the money comes in.

Teams of American industrial divers are currently inspecting the hulls of the floating terminals to check that they haven't been sabotaged.

AmeriCorp 's IT teams replaced all the control systems. **PetroVen 's old computers** were ripped out and replaced with servers connected via **OrbitalLink satellite** directly to Houston. In less than a week, the "brain" of Venezuelan exports had relocated to Texas.

The "Supply Chain" Express

The port of Houston has opened a "Venezuelan Corridor." Supply ships depart every six hours. They receive a complete exemption from customs duties upon arrival.

It's an influx of equipment. Kilometers of flexible hoses, thousands of new valves, and submersible pumps are arriving. The image is striking: American technicians in new protective suits are installing state-of-the-art equipment in the middle of oil fields that resemble open-air dumps.

The Role of the "Vultures" of Maintenance

An entire sub-industry is rubbing its hands together: service companies specializing in "Revamping".

Companies like **StormFord Services** or **Hughes Drilling** have signed "Cost-Plus" contracts to audit each well.

Their method is binary: they don't seek to optimize the deposit for the long term (which would be in Venezuela's interest), they seek immediate *cash flow (the interest of the USA). It's a high-grading* strategy

.

4. The Great Divide: Yalta in the Orinoco

One of the myths of liberalism is free and undistorted competition. Under the "Houston Plan," competition was abolished in favor of a cartelized distribution of territories.

Venezuela is sliced up like a birthday cake.

"AmeriCorpistan" (The West and the Western Belt)

AmeriCorp is the big winner. Having maintained a continuous presence in the country through OFAC licenses, AmeriCorp knows the territory.

- **The Booty:** They are credited with almost total control of the Maracaibo Basin and the most productive blocks of the Orinoco Belt.
- **The Logic:** They already have the logistics infrastructure in place. Their mission is to provide immediate cash flow.

The Return of the King: Titan Energy (The Eastern Belt and Offshore)

Titan Energy had left Venezuela in a huff in 2007. The return is a cold act of revenge.

- **The Spoils:** Titan claims — and obtains — the Eastern Belt blocks (the former **EuroEnergy** and **Britannic Oil projects** , abandoned). But above all, Titan takes control of **offshore exploration** on the border with Guyana.
- **The Strategy:** Titan is already massively exploiting oil in

neighboring Guyana. By acquiring the adjacent Venezuelan waters, Titan is geologically unifying the basin.

The Europeans' Consolation Prize

Washington is pragmatic. To avoid the European Union crying foul about an imperialist monopoly, it's necessary to leave crumbs for its allies.

- **Iberia Petróleo** (Spain) and **Romana Energy** (Italy): These companies have their rights to the gas fields confirmed. Gas is less strategic for the US than heavy oil. Europeans have the right to produce gas... to fuel the power plants that will run the American oil pumps.

The Exclusion Zone (The Asian Purge)

The most critical point concerns the assets of **SinoOil** (China) and **Volga Oil** (Russia).

Venezuela had ceded vast territories to these powers in exchange for loans. The "Houston Plan" is radical: these contracts are declared **"null and void** . "

- **The Legal Argument:** American lawyers argue that these contracts were never constitutionally ratified.
- **The Physical Reality: SinoOil** engineers were evicted from the fields by military police. These blocks are placed under the "provisional administration" of an American consortium (**Phillips-Conrad**) pending a new bidding process.

5. Legal Engineering: The "Lex America"

Once the territory is divided, the system must be secured by law. The problem is that the Venezuelan Constitution enshrines public ownership of the subsoil.

For Americans, this is unacceptable. No *major oil company* will invest $20 billion if it has to obey a **PetroVen bureaucrat** .

The lawyers at **Botts Legal** and **Case & Black** therefore drafted the **"Emergency Energy Reconstruction Decree"** .

The end of the Empresa Mixta

The decree introduces a new legal vehicle: the **Independent Production Agreement (IPA)** .

- *In theory:* The state retains ownership of the oil "in the subsoil".
- *In practice:* As soon as the oil passes the wellhead, it becomes the property of the private operator.
- *Control:* The State no longer holds shares in the company. It only has the right to collect royalties.

Sovereign Immunity

The most humiliating clause is that of jurisdiction.

Any dispute between the Venezuelan state and American companies will not be adjudicated by the courts of Caracas, but by the courts of **New York** or international arbitration.

If Venezuela ever wants to raise taxes, **Titan Energy** could take the state to court in Manhattan.

6. Financial Slavery: The "Fideicomiso" Model

If the law controls the land, who controls the money?

The "Houston Plan" learned from past mistakes. Washington trusts no one.

The major innovation is the total financial control of the country via the **Trust Account** (Fideicomiso) mechanism.

The Dollar Circuit

Here's how the Venezuelan oil economy will function from February 2026:

1. **Extraction: AmeriCorp** extracts a barrel of oil.
2. **Sale : AmeriCorp sells this barrel to an Alamo Refining**

refinery in Texas.

3. **Collection:** The money is **not** transferred to the Central Bank of Venezuela. It is transferred to a "Venezuela Reconstruction Account" held at the **Federal Reserve Bank of New York** .

The Distribution Algorithm

This account in New York is managed by a joint committee. The money is distributed according to a strict priority:

- **Priority 1 (Private Debt Service):** Reimbursement of the operating costs of oil companies (**Titan** , **AmeriCorp**). They take their share first.
- **Priority 2 (Selective Sovereign Debt):** Payment to Western creditors (funds like **Onyx Capital**).
- **Priority 3:** Purchase of food and goods... supplied by American companies such as **AgriCorp** and **Midwest Grain** .
- **Priority 4:** The remainder (if any) is transferred to the Venezuelan government to pay civil servants.

7. Political Theatre: "Sign or Die"

Cayena Hotel, Caracas. January 21, 2026.

Representatives of the new Venezuelan government are hesitant to sign this Faustian pact.

The American Special Envoy lays down an ultimatum:

"Gentlemen, tankers filled with refined gasoline and diesel are waiting offshore, sent by ***Alamo Refining*** *and* ***Spartan Downstream*** *. They can dock tomorrow and get the country going again."*

But these tankers will only dock once the new legal framework is signed. No signature, no fuel. Without fuel, your government falls in 48 hours. Sign the law, and we'll open the floodgates.

This is humanitarian blackmail. Energy is being used as a weapon of diplomatic persuasion.

The Venezuelan delegates, with their backs to the wall, sign. They know they are selling out the future to secure the present.

The decree was published on the night of January 22nd.

The next morning, the first American tankers entered the port of La Guaira. **PetroVen** is dead. Long live **VenAm Oil** .

Venezuela is no longer an oil-producing country. It is an oil-producing territory under foreign administration.

A. The Convoy of Fear: Road to the East

Gran Mariscal Highway of Ayacucho , State of Miranda. January 25, 2026.

Jack "The Hammer" O'Neil hated this road. A former project manager for **Burton & Hall** in Iraq and Libya, he thought he'd seen it all. But Venezuela had a particular smell: a mixture of cheap gasoline, decaying tropical vegetation, and urban squalor.

Sentinel Global security agents . In front and behind them, three other identical vehicles formed the convoy. In the sky, a surveillance drone buzzed overhead, piloted from the US base at the airport.

His mission was simple on paper, but suicidal in reality: to go to the José petrochemical complex, 250 kilometers east of Caracas, to "take possession" of the assets on behalf of the American consortium.

"We have a roadblock ahead," announced the driver, a former member of the Colombian Special Forces, with Olympian calm.

O'Neil looked through the tinted window. It wasn't a military roadblock. It was a barricade made of burning tires and bus carcasses. About fifty men, some armed with machetes, others with old pistols, were blocking the road. "Are they Chavistas?" O'Neil asked.

"Worse," replied the head of security. "Hungry residents. They want to see what's in the trucks behind us."

The convoy was carrying electric generators and MRE food rations for the engineers' living quarters. A fortune for the starving crowd.

"Shall we force our way through?" asked the driver.

O'Neil thought for a moment. If they opened fire, there would be a riot. And CNN was somewhere in the area. — No. Open the window. Give me the megaphone.

O'Neil, who spoke a construction-site Spanish learned in Mexico, lowered the window a few centimeters.

" Listen *!* " I'm an engineer. I'm here to get the plant running again. If the plant is running, there's work. If you block us, nobody eats."

A man approached, shirtless, a machete in his hand.

"We don't care about the work, Gringo. We want what's in the truck." O'Neil sighed. He pulled a wad of greenbacks from his pocket. Physical dollars, not crypto. Real Benjamin Franklins.

— There's $5,000 here. That's for the "toll." Let us through, and I'll hire you tomorrow morning to clean the perimeter of the factory. Paid in dollars.

The man looked at the money, then at the heavily armed convoy. He took the wad of cash. He waved his hand. The barricade opened.

O'Neil rolled up the window.

"Note that in the expenses," he told his deputy. "Community relations expenses." That was the first lesson of reconstruction: the dollar was more powerful than the M4. But you needed a lot of it.

B. The Encounter: Texas Confronts Socialism

José Industrial Complex. 4 hours later.

The complex was a ghost town of rusted pipes and silent distillation towers. No smoke, no noise. Just the sea breeze.

O'Neil got out of the vehicle. He was greeted not by an army, but by a lone woman, standing in front of the dilapidated administrative building.

She was wearing a yellowed white construction helmet and a shirt with the faded **PetroVen logo** .

"I'm Elena Rodriguez, chief operations engineer," she said in English. Or at least, what was left of it.

O'Neil adjusted his sunglasses.

— Jack O'Neil, **Burton & Hall** . I am the new administrator appointed by the VRA. Where is the plant manager?

"He left in a private jet for Miami three days ago with the slush fund," Elena replied without emotion.

— And the engineers?

— Gone. Or taxi drivers in Caracas.

— Who runs the show?

— Me. And a team of twenty technicians who haven't been paid for six months. We slept here to prevent looters from stealing the copper cables.

O'Neil looked at the woman. She was thin, with dark circles under her eyes, but her eyes burned with a cold pride. She had protected the billion-dollar asset with nothing but her will.

"Why did you stay?" O'Neil asked.

"Because this is my country, Gringo. And because I know that without this factory, Venezuela dies. You came to steal the oil, I know that. But to steal it, you need it to be flowing. So, we have a common interest."

O'Neil smiled. He liked that kind of pragmatism.

— Okay, Elena. Show me the control room. We have work to do.

C. The Inventory of Horror: The "Cemetery of the Vannes"

What they discovered inside surpassed O'Neil's worst nightmares.

The "Houston Plan" had indeed provided for repairs. But it had planned to repair a damaged factory, not one that had been cannibalized.

In the turbine room, O'Neil stopped, stunned.

The three giant Siemens turbines, needed to compress the gas, were there. But they were open like gutted fish.

"Where are the rotors?" O'Neil yelled.

"Sold," Elena said calmly.

— Sold? To whom?

— To an Iranian scrap dealer last year. The manager needed money to pay for his daughter's birthday party. He sold the titanium alloy rotors by weight.

O'Neil ran his hand over his face.

— Do you know how long it takes to order a rotor of this type from Germany? Eighteen months!

"That's why we need your parts," Elena said.

— This isn't maintenance, it's industrial archaeology!

They continued the inspection. Everywhere, the same observation.

The pumps no longer had seals. The control computers (old PCs running Windows XP) had been stolen. The pressure sensors had been replaced with pieces of tape with marker notes reading: *"Do not touch, it leaks"* .

In the director's office, O'Neil set up his headquarters. He took out his **OrbitalLink satellite phone** and called headquarters in Houston.

— Hello, Bill? It's Jack. Listen to me carefully. Forget the 500 million budget. — What? It's going to cost more?

— Bill, there's no factory. There's just an empty shell. We have to rebuild everything. The pipes, the pumps, the electronics. Everything.

— Shit, Jack. The shareholders are going to scream.

"No, Bill, think about it. It's a *cost-plus contract* . The more we spend, the more we earn. It's a jackpot. I'm going to need three truckloads of equipment by Monday. And send me 50 engineers. Not interns. Guys who know how to weld under fire. We're essentially remaking the Marshall Plan, but with a 15% margin."

He hung up. Elena was looking at him. She understood.

"You're not going to repair it," she said. "You're going to replace it."

— Exactly. In six months, this factory will be a **Burton & Hall factory** . Not a single Venezuelan bolt will remain.

— And what about us?

— You, Elena, have just tripled your salary. Welcome to capitalism.

D. The Traitors' Dinner: The Carving Out

While O'Neil was dealing with the rust on the pitch, another scene was playing out in the air-conditioned suites of the Marriott Hotel in Caracas. It was the scene where sovereignty changed hands, not with wrenches, but with Montblanc pens.

Presidential Suite, Marriott Hotel. January 27, 2026.

Around the coffee table, three men:

1. **James Sterling** , the legal director of **Titan Energy** .
2. **General "El Flaco"** , a former high-ranking Chavista who had switched sides 24 hours before the invasion and now controlled security in the oil zone.
3. **Dr. Velasquez** , the new acting Minister of Petroleum, a terrified technocrat who hadn't slept for three days.

Sterling placed a thick, 200-page document on the table.

— This is the Independent Production Agreement (IPA) for the Junín 4 block, known as Sterling.

Velasquez took the document. His hands were trembling.

"I've read the draft," he said in a weak voice. "Article 4... you 're asking for a 30-year tax exemption? That's illegal according to our constitution."

Sterling smiled, a shark's smile.

— Dr. Velasquez, your constitution is a charming document, but it doesn't pay your army's wages. Currently, your ministry's bank account is empty. Zero. If you don't sign it tonight, tomorrow morning the General here won't be able to pay his men. And I wouldn't bet on your survival if the Praetorian Guard isn't paid. Isn't that right, General?

General "El Flaco," sitting in the shadows, lit a cigar. He wore a solid gold Rolex, a recent gift from his new friends.

— The Gringo is right, Minister. My men are nervous. They need to know the money is coming. Sign.

"But that's a surrender!" protested Velasquez. "You're taking 80% of the profit!" "We're taking 80% of the *risk* ," corrected Sterling. "We're putting up the money. We're putting up the technology. You're putting up the land. It's a good deal."

Sterling leaned forward.

— Listen, Velasquez. We can do this nicely. You sign, you become the hero who brought in the foreign investment. We've planned a $5 million Signing Bonus, paid into a numbered account in Dubai, for... " consulting fees ."

Velasquez froze.

"Or," Sterling continued, "we can find another minister. There are plenty of young guns in the opposition who would kill to sit in your chair."

The silence lasted a minute. The hum of the air conditioning and police sirens could be heard in the distance in Caracas.

Velasquez looked at the General. The General nodded, absently tapping his pistol holster.

Velasquez looked at the contract. He looked at Sterling.

— Where do I sign?

Sterling handed him his pen.

At that precise moment, the Junín 4 block — containing 40 billion barrels of oil, more than the total reserves of Qatar — ceased to belong to Venezuela and became an asset in the consolidated balance sheet of **Titan Energy** , based in Irving, Texas.

E. The First Barrel: The Bitter Victory

José's Terminal. February 15, 2026.

Three weeks later. Jack O'Neil stood on the loading dock. He had lost 5 kilos, he was covered in grease stains and mosquito bites, but he had made it.

Behind him, the supertanker *Titan Pride* was moored.

The pumps, repaired with cannibalized parts and urgently imported equipment, roared.

Elena Rodriguez was beside him. She watched the vibrating black pipe. Oil was flowing. The first post-war shipment.

— 2 million barrels, said O'Neil. Heading to Louisiana.

"It's our blood that's leaving," Elena murmured.

— It's business, Elena. It's just business.

O'Neil picked up his radio.

— Control room, this is O'Neil. Maximum flow. Fill it to the brim.

The ship sank gently into the water under the weight of the cargo.

Sentinel Global security agents stood guard with assault rifles.

In the distance, on the hill overlooking the terminal, O'Neil saw a column of black smoke. A village was burning. Probably an army clearing operation to secure the area.

"We did a good job," said O'Neil, turning his back on the smoke.

He didn't yet know that this oil, which he had struggled so hard to extract, would trigger a global financial war. He didn't know that every barrel loaded onto that tanker was a drop of poison for the American economy.

For now, he was just an engineer who had finished his job.

He took out his phone.

— Hello, Houston? The tap is open. You can notify Wall Street.

CHAPTER 3: DISGUISED PRIVATIZATION

The end of oil nationalism and the advent of the corporate state.

Headquarters of PetroVen (formerly PDVSA), La Campiña, Caracas. February 2, 2026.

The smell has changed. It's the first thing the surviving employees notice as they pass through the security turnstiles of the La Campiña complex. For twenty years, the corridors of the national company's headquarters (now rebranded as **PetroVen** in official U.S. communications) smelled of stale coffee, the cold sweat of malfunctioning air conditioners, and, metaphorically, political fear. Today, they smell of lemon-scented industrial disinfectant and fresh paint.

In the main hall, the enormous portrait of Hugo Chávez, which had overlooked the atrium since his death in 2013, is gone. It hasn't been replaced by a portrait of the new interim president, nor by an American flag—that would be too crude. It has been replaced by a gigantic high-definition LED screen that continuously displays stock market charts, the real-time price of WTI crude oil, and slogans in English and Spanish: "Efficiency, Transparency, Safety."

This is the new mantra. The era of "Oil Sovereignty" is dead. The era of "Operational Performance" begins.

This chapter is not about geology, but about ideology. It recounts how, in the space of a few weeks, the largest public company in Latin America was stripped of its political substance and transformed into a legal shell serving private capital, under the control of giants like **AmeriCorp Petroleum** and **Titan Energy** . It is the story of the transformation of the Venezuelan citizen into an exploitable "human resource."

1. The Semantics of Theft: How Not to Say "Privatization"

The first obstacle to American control was not military, but constitutional. Article 302 of the Venezuelan Constitution reserves oil activity for the State, *"for reasons of national sovereignty ." The word "privatization" is radioactive.*

So, lawyers in Houston and spin doctors in Washington have invented a new jargon. Instead of privatization, they're talking about **"Strategic Recovery Partnerships" (SRPs)** .

The "Full Delegation" mechanism

Under the old system, *Empresas Mixtas* gave 51% of their shares to the State. The new model, implemented from February 2026, reverses this logic without altering nominal ownership:

1. **The property remains public:** On paper, **PetroVen** still owns 100% of the reserves. The honor of the nationalists is preserved.
2. **The operation is 100% private:** Through a "Risk Service" contract, **PetroVen** delegates *all* operations to the foreign operator.
3. **The Right of Veto:** The crucial innovation is the elimination of the state's right to oversee day-to-day operations. **AmeriCorp** or **Titan Energy** decide independently where to drill, which company to subcontract, and who to hire.

In practical terms, the Venezuelan state is downgraded from the status of "Owner-Operator" to that of passive "Owner-Renter." It receives a check at the end of the month (the royalties), but is forbidden from entering the engine room.

2. The Great Purge: Human Resources as a Weapon of War

If the legal structures change, so do the people. **PetroVen** officially had 140,000 employees in 2025. According to **Titan Energy audits** , only 30,000 were needed for actual production.

During the first week of February, a terrible scene unfolded outside the human resources offices. Employees were not being fired by humans, but by a software program. The databases had been cross-referenced with those of the *Carnet de la Patria (Patria's Notebook*).

Three categories of personnel were created, identified by the color of their new access badge:

1. **Blacklist (The "Excluded"):** All those who have held a position of political or union responsibility. For them, it's immediate dismissal, without compensation. This affects approximately 90,000 people. Overnight, an army of unemployed is thrown into the streets.
2. **Grey List (The "Probationary" Staff):** Lower-level technicians. They are kept on, but with a new, precarious 3-month contract. They must sign a "Political Neutrality" charter that prohibits any strikes.
3. **Blue List (The "Repatriates"):** The new elite. These are overwhelmingly Venezuelans from the diaspora (Miami, Houston) who are returning to the country.

The Culture Clash of the "Miami Boys"

The return of the diaspora creates explosive social tension.

The "Repatriates" arrive with new clothes and technocratic arrogance. They are paid in dollars into offshore accounts , while the locals are paid in local currency.

This isn't a team merger, it's internal colonization. They're forcing local senior engineers, who have 20 years of field experience, to take basic training courses taught by 25-year-old kids sent by **AmeriCorp** .

3. The End of the State within a State

Under Chávez and Maduro, the national company was the ministry of everything: food, housing, health.

On February 10, a circular memo, drafted by the consulting firm **Kinsey & Partners** (mandated for the restructuring), was issued: *"As of* *today, all expenditure not directly related to the exploration, production, refining or distribution of hydrocarbons is permanently suspended."*

The consequences are immediate:

- **The People's Canteens:** Food distribution networks are closing.
- **Clinics:** Company-funded health clinics in oil areas are no longer receiving medicines.

The response of the new American administrators to the protests was one of pure economic cynicism: *"Our role is to generate profit. With that profit, the Venezuelan state will be able—if it manages it well—to build houses."*

The Venezuelan social safety net was replaced by a void.

4. The Archipelago: The Geography of Segregation

To guarantee the security and effectiveness of American operations, it is necessary to create bubbles. This is the concept of **the "Oil Archipelago"** .

In Puerto La Cruz and Punta de Mata, veritable forbidden cities are emerging. Concrete walls isolate the facilities.

Inside **AmeriCorp bases** : running drinking water, 24/7 electricity, supermarkets stocked with imported goods (**K-Cereal** , **Keystone Foods** , **American Cola** **), and** high-speed

OrbitalLink satellite internet . Outside: slums, power outages, and insecurity.

This segregation creates a deep-seated hatred. Americans are no longer seen as liberators, but as a caste of occupiers living in luxury amidst misery.

5. The Case of Auxiliary Industry: The Death of Local SMEs

Venezuela had a network of small and medium-sized oil service companies. The "Houston Plan" abolished national preference in the name of "quality."

The new contracts stipulated that all suppliers must be certified according to the latest ISO standards and have insurance with an "A" rated insurer such as **The London Syndicate** .

99% of Venezuelan companies cannot meet these criteria.

As a result, subcontracting contracts go to companies based in Houston, which open a "mailbox" subsidiary in Caracas.

- Who repairs the pipelines? A subsidiary of **Burton & Hall** .
- Who supplies the food? A subsidiary of **AgriCorp** .
-

  Oil money makes a round trip: extracted from Venezuelan soil, and immediately sent back to the USA.

6. Case Study: The Paraguaná Refinery (CRP)

To illustrate this transformation, let's zoom in on the *Centro de Refinación Paraguaná* (CRP).

After (March 2026) - Under Operation Alamo Refining:

The entrance to the complex resembles a NATO checkpoint.

Alamo Refining engineers decided not to repair everything. They condemned 60% of the refinery, deeming it too old. They are focusing solely on the units capable of producing naphtha for export.

The goal is no longer to produce gasoline for the Venezuelan market. The goal is to produce semi-finished products for refineries in Texas. Venezuela is losing its capacity to produce its own refined gasoline. It is becoming structurally dependent on imports from the USA to fuel its vehicles.

7. The Resistance of the Nuts

José Terminal, Anzoategui State. March 14, 2026.

At 3:42 a.m., a piercing alarm pierced the night. The pressure in the 36-inch pipeline carrying crude oil to the ship *Texas Star* had just dropped.

Someone had manually loosened the bolts on the number 404 flange connection. The bolts were gone.

This incident marks the beginning of the "**Resistance of the Nuts**" . The euphoria of reconstruction is over.

The Death of the Syndicate

As early as February 2026, the emergency decree dissolved the powerful Chavista union. In its place, **AmeriCorp 's HR departments** implemented **"Consultative Works Councils** ," modeled after the anti-union American system. The word "strike" was banned.

The Typology of Passive Sabotage

Since anger cannot be expressed vertically, it becomes lateral.

1. **The Decimal Point Error:** A lab technician makes a mistake in analyzing viscosity. The oil is spilled in Texas. Cost: $5 million.
2. **The Missing Piece:** Critical parts are mislabeled in the warehouse.

   It's a reverse work-to-rule. Venezuela becomes the world champion of "passive resistance."

8. The "Malinchisist" Dilemma

In the midst of this industrial cold war are Venezuelan middle managers, like **"Roberto"** , a production engineer.

He hated Maduro and wanted to rebuild his country. But at work, he was humiliated by his American boss at **Titan Energy** who didn't listen to him.

When he returns home, his neighbors call him a *Malinchist* (collaborator).

Roberto and his colleagues live in a state of permanent cognitive dissonance. They are the well-oiled cogs in a machine that is crushing their own national identity.

9. Militarization (Praetorian & Sentinel)

Faced with sabotage, the oil *majors* have responded by escalating security measures.

Oil sites are managed like forward operating bases.

Since the Venezuelan police are considered corrupt, security has been privatized. Companies like **Praetorian Group** (formerly Blackwater) and **Sentinel Global** have landed lucrative contracts.

Their men patrol in combat gear inside the refineries themselves. The atmosphere is prison-like: strip searches, ban on phones, random lie detectors.

AmeriCorp has installed an AI system called *"Overwatch"* : facial recognition cameras monitor the production lines. If two workers talk for too long, an alert is sent.

It is estimated that the security budget now represents **15 to 20% of operational costs** (OPEX). Venezuelan oil is cheap to extract, but very expensive to protect.

10. The Ecological Dead End: The "Dirty" Secret

In the race to repay the debt, the environment is sacrificed.

The order from Houston is clear: *"Liquid first. Gas is waste."*

Venezuela in 2026 lights up at night. Billions of cubic meters of gas are *flared* .

For toxic production wastewater, since the injection wells are sealed, it is discreetly discharged into rivers. The legal immunity negotiated in the "Houston Plan" protects **Titan Energy** and **AmeriCorp** from any local environmental lawsuits.

A. The Morning of the Long Knives: The Purge Algorithm

PetroVen Tower, La Campiña, Caracas. February 8, 2026. 7:30 a.m.

It was a gray and stifling Monday morning. Gustavo Mendez, 54, a senior geologist specializing in the stratigraphy of heavy sediments, approached the tempered glass security gates. He had worked in this tower since 1998. He had survived the 2002 coup, the oil strike, the death of Chávez, and Maduro's hyperinflation. He thought he could outlast the Americans. After all, he knew the rock better than anyone.

He presented his magnetic badge to the reader.

Usually, the indicator light would turn green with a discreet beep.

That morning, the reader emitted a low hum and lit up in **RED** .

The screen displayed a single word: **ACCESS DENIED - CODE 99** .

Gustavo frowned. He tried again. Red beep.

He looked around. He wasn't alone. In the vast hall, about fifty other employees — secretaries, accountants, maintenance engineers — were stuck in front of the barriers, looking bewildered.

"It's a computer error," Gustavo said aloud, trying to reassure himself. "They changed the system this weekend."

PetroVen security uniform , but a black tactical uniform with the **Sentinel Global logo** . He was tall, muscular, and didn't speak Spanish. He was holding a tablet.

— *Name?* the guard barked .

— Mendez. Gustavo Mendez. Department of Geology.

The guard tapped on his tablet. He didn't even look Gustavo in the eye. "Code 99. You are on the political dismissal list. Please hand in your badge and leave the building immediately."

Gustavo felt the ground give way beneath him.

"Politics? I've never been involved in politics! I'm a scientist! I only have my party card because we were required to have it to receive meal vouchers!" The guard gestured. Two other mercenaries approached, hands on their tasers. "Sir, please don't make a scene. Your belongings will be mailed to you. Please leave."

At the same time, a group of young people entered the hall. They wore tailored suits, shiny Italian shoes, and **BLUE badges** around their necks. They were laughing and speaking a mixture of English and Spanish with a Miami drawl.

" *Check this out* ," one of them said. "This lobby is *so 80s* . We're going to have to redo everything."

They passed through the security gates. Their badges beeped green.

Gustavo recognized one of them. He was the son of a former director who had fled to Florida in 2005. The kid was 25. He'd probably never seen an oil well in his life. But he had the right name, the right American degree, and the right color badge.

Gustavo, the geologist with 30 years of experience, was pushed toward the revolving door by the **Sentinel guard** . Outside, on the sidewalk, hundreds of other "Code 99" employees were weeping or screaming with rage. The company's memory had just been thrown out onto the street.

B. The Hunger Auditor: The End of the Missions

Neighborhood 23 of Enero , West of Caracas. February 12, 2026.

Sarah Jenkins hated this part of the job. A junior consultant at **Kinsey & Partners** , she was a Harvard graduate and thought she was coming to Venezuela to do macroeconomic strategy. Instead, she found herself in the back of an armored SUV, escorted by paramilitaries, auditing "social cost centers."

Barrio network of medical clinics

Adentro , historically funded by **PetroVen** .

The clinic was a small brick house painted blue, in the middle of narrow alleyways. Inside, a queue of fifty people. Mothers with feverish babies, elderly diabetics.

The doctor, an exhausted Venezuelan (the Cuban doctors had been expelled the first week), welcomed him with hope.

"Are you bringing the insulin?" he asked, seeing the American logo on Sarah's file. "We've been out of it for ten days."

Sarah adjusted her glasses. She opened her laptop.

— No, Doctor. I'm here to take inventory. We need to determine if this center is "Core Business" for the company's new strategy.

She began to ask cold, mechanical questions.

— How many patients per day? What is the average cost per treatment? Do you have a billing system?

The doctor looked at her as if she were from Mars.

— Billing? It's free, Madam. They're poor. They can't pay. **PetroVen** pays. That's the social contract. Oil pays for healthcare.

Sarah sighed. She typed a note into her Excel column: *"Business model not viable. Recovery rate: 0%. Recommendation: Immediate closure."*

She closed her computer.

— Doctor, I'm sorry. According to new performance criteria imposed by the **Titan/AmeriCorp consortium** , philanthropic activities are suspended. This center will close on Friday.

"But where will they go?" asked the doctor, pointing to the queue. "The transitional government will probably put in place another system," said Sarah, reciting talking points learned at the briefing. "We run an oil company, not a hospital."

As they were leaving, an old woman grabbed Sarah's arm.

— *Gringa* , my husband is dying without his pills. Help us.

The security guard violently pushed the old woman away.

— Don't touch the staff!

Sarah got into the SUV. She put on her noise-canceling headphones so she wouldn't hear the screams.

"Take me back to the Marriott," she told the driver. "I need a shower." On her screen, the "Enero Dispensary 23" line changed from "Active" to "Liquidated." She had just saved the company $5,000 a month.

And to probably sentence ten people to death.

C. The Clash of Worlds: The "Sifrino" and the Foreman

Carabobo Oil Field, Orinoco Belt. February 20, 2026.

The tension under the command tent was palpable. The portable air conditioner struggled against the 40-degree heat, but failed to cool tempers.

On one side of the table sat Ricardo "Ricky" Valdes, 28, an MBA graduate from Rice University in Houston. He wore a pristine **AmeriCorp polo shirt** , an Apple Watch Ultra, and smelled of expensive cologne. He was a "Sifrino" (a rich kid), fresh from Miami in the army. He was the new "Area Supervisor."

On the other side was Mateo, 55 years old. His skin was tanned like leather, his hands covered in indelible oil stains. He wore dirty orange overalls. He was the local foreman. He knew every pipe in this field by its first name.

"I don't understand why you're questioning my orders," said Ricky in English, refusing to speak Spanish on principle of "corporate culture."

Mateo replied in Spanish, slowly, with contempt.

"Because if we inject steam at that pressure, like your American manual says, we'll fracture the reservoir. The rock here is brittle. This isn't Texas, kid. Here, the crude oil is viscous like molasses. We have to go slowly." The interpreter translated. Ricky rolled his eyes.

— Listen, Mateo. I have the numerical simulations done in Houston. They say 1,500 PSI. We have to reach production quotas to pay off the debt. If you don't increase the pressure, you'll slow down the cash flow.

"If I turn up the pressure, I'll break the well! And we'll lose six months!" Mateo yelled. "Am I the boss, or are you?" Ricky interrupted . "You're paid to turn the valve, not to think. Your old-fashioned methods are over. We want efficiency."

Mateo stood up. He approached Ricky.

— Do you know how much I get paid, "Chief"?

Ricky stepped back slightly, intimidated by the foreman's physical bulk. — This is confidential.

— No, it's not confidential. I get paid 120 *Libertad Coins* a month. That's 60 real dollars. You get 15,000 dollars a month plus your risk bonus. And you want to teach me my job?

Ricky pressed the button on his radio.

— Security, come to the command tent. I have an insubordinate employee. Two Colombian guards from **Sentinel Global** entered.

— Escort the gentleman off the premises. He has been dismissed for incompetence and refusal to obey orders. Take away his Grey badge.

Mateo spat on the ground, right next to Ricky's new Timberland boots.

"You're going to break this well, kid. And when it breaks, don't come looking for me."

Mateo left with his head held high. Ricky wiped his forehead.

"Incredible," he said to his American deputy. "These people are unmanageable. They are lazy and arrogant."

He turned towards the computer.

— Increase the pressure to 1500 PSI.

Three days later, the casing of well C-45 exploded under pressure, causing a massive crude oil spill and a two-week production shutdown. In his report, Ricky blamed "sabotage by Chavista employees."

D. The Las Mercedes Bubble: Champagne and Misery

Restaurant "Le Brut", Las Mercedes district, Caracas. Saturday evening.

The contrast was obscene. Outside, Caracas was plunged into one of those chronic blackouts. The city was a black, silent, and terrifying mass, punctuated only by the headlights of military patrols.

But inside the Las Mercedes security perimeter, the industrial generators hummed. The lights shone.

At the restaurant "Le Brut", the new canteen for expatriates and the elites of the reconstruction, the atmosphere was festive.

Titan Energy executives were drinking $25 martinis. At a table, a

Kinsey consultant was explaining to a Miami construction contractor how to overcharge for concrete.

— The trick is to charge for "secure transport". You buy the bag of cement for 5 bucks, you charge 50 bucks for armored logistics. The VRA pays without question.

In one corner, Ricky (the supervisor who had fired Mateo) was having dinner with a Venezuelan model . They were eating Wagyu beef imported from Japan.

"It's crazy how the city is changing," Ricky was saying. "There's a new energy. You can feel business picking up."

The girl smiled, but her eyes were sad. She came from a poor neighborhood. She was there because it was the only way to pay for her mother's medication.

"Yes," she said. "There is money."

"You know," Ricky continued, "the hardest thing is changing mindsets. The locals... they're dependent. They expect the state to give them everything. We bring them a culture of hard work."

He signaled to the waiter.

— Another bottle of Dom Pérignon, please. And put it on the "Representation" expense report.

On the other side of the bulletproof glass, in the dark street, a ten-year-old boy was rummaging through the restaurant's garbage. He found half a Wagyu steak, barely touched. He devoured it greedily.

A private security guard came out and kicked him out.

Inside, no one saw the scene. The music was too loud.

E. The Birth of Sabotage: The First Bolt

José's terminal. The same night.

Mateo, the fired foreman, hadn't gone home. He'd drunk a bottle of cheap rum with his former colleagues, those who were still on the "Grey List" and worked the night shift.

They were sitting on the beach, watching the lights of the terminal where the Americans were loading oil.

"They broke well C-45," Mateo recounted. "I told them so."

"They don't care," replied a welder. "They're insured."

"It's not fair," Mateo murmured. "It's our oil. It's our sweat. And they treat us like dogs."

The welder took an adjustable wrench out of his pocket. He twisted it in his hand.

"You know, Mateo... the new automatic valve system they installed on pipeline 4?"

- Yes ?

— I noticed something. They removed the manual vibration sensors to install their crappy Wi-Fi system. But the Wi-Fi signal doesn't work well behind hangar 3. There's a dead zone.

Mateo looked at his friend. He understood.

— A gray area?

— Yes. For about 15 meters. If someone... let's say, loosened the bolts on the main flange just a little... the system wouldn't detect it right away. The pressure would build, and boom. A nasty leak. It would cost them a fortune in delay penalties for the ship.

Mateo picked up the bottle of rum. He took a long swig. He thought about Ricky's humiliation. He thought about his 30-year career wiped out by a kid from Miami. He thought about the severance pay he'd never received.

He took the wrench from the welder's hands.

— Hangar 3, you say?

— Hangar 3. Between 2 and 3 a.m., the **Sentinel patrol** takes a coffee break.

Mateo got up. He wasn't staggering. He was perfectly lucid.

— I'm just going to... go for a walk. To see if the Wi-Fi is working.

That night, Mateo only loosened one bolt. It wasn't much. Just a warning.

But this gesture, repeated by thousands of other humiliated Mateos across the country, would become the grain of sand that jammed the most powerful economic war machine in the world. The resistance was not born of a political ideology. It was born of the wounded pride of a competent man treated like a slave.

Conclusion

From a macroeconomic perspective, it's a success: production is rebounding.

From a micro-social perspective, it's a ticking time bomb. Society is fractured, the productive apparatus is sabotaged from within, and the land is poisoned. The United States has built an oil fortress in the middle of an ocean of hostility. And meanwhile, outside, China is preparing its financial retaliation.

CHAPTER 4: THE DEBT WAR AND THE DRAGON'S RETALIATION The doctrine of the "Armed Dollar" and the silent partitioning of the world.

Zhongnanhai (Residence of Party Leaders), Beijing. January 25, 2026.

It's snowing in the Forbidden City. Inside the ultra-secure complex housing the elite of the Chinese Communist Party, the atmosphere is as icy as the air outside. The Politburo Standing Committee is meeting in an extraordinary session.

On the table was a 50-page report prepared by the Ministry of State Security (MSS) and the **Bank of Beijing Development** (formerly CDB). The title was understated: *"Assessment of Strategic Losses Following Imperialist Aggression in Venezuela* . "

The figures are staggering. Between 2007 and 2024, China loaned approximately $62 billion to Venezuela. By the time of the US invasion, the total exposure (loans + investments in joint ventures) was approaching **$25 billion** .

The problem isn't the money, but the **precedent** . If Washington succeeds in erasing this debt with the stroke of a legal pen, by declaring the loans granted to Maduro illegitimate, then the entire "Belt and Road Initiative" collapses.

The Chinese President gives the order to retaliate: *"We will demonstrate to them that a barrel of illegally extracted oil is unsellable. Activate Operation 'Financial Scorched Earth'."*

1. Washington's Offensive: The "Odious Debt" Doctrine

To understand the Chinese response, one must first analyze the American attack.

From the moment the transitional government was established in Caracas, lawyers from the firm **Cleary & Moore** , advisors to the new

Venezuelan government (and paid by the US State Department), resurrected the **Doctrine of Odious Debt** .

This theory stipulates that a debt incurred by a despotic regime to consolidate its power is not a state debt, but a personal debt of the regime.

On January 28, 2026, the Venezuelan Minister of Finance declared in New York:

"The billions loaned by China were used to maintain a dictatorship. The Venezuelan people should not have to repay their debts. We declare the debt to the ***Bank of Beijing Development*** *as 'odious' and void."*

Simultaneously, the IMF, under American pressure, classifies Chinese debt as **commercial** and not sovereign debt, allowing it to lend money to Venezuela despite the default on payment to Beijing.

2. The Dragon's Counterattack: Legal Asymmetry

China does not recognize New York's jurisdiction. It is adopting the strategy of "vulture funds" like **Apex Management** . If Venezuela does not pay, China will seize all Venezuelan assets outside of the United States.

On February 5, 2026, the trap closes in Rotterdam.

The supertanker *"Simon Bolivar* ," operated by the new pro-US administration, enters the Dutch port. No sooner has it docked than bailiffs seize the ship at the request of **SinoOil** (the Chinese oil company). The reason: breach of commercial contract.

The tanker is stuck. The message is clear: *"You can extract the oil, but you will not be able to sell it outside the US market."*

Within a week, similar actions were launched in Singapore and Portugal. The Western legal system began to falter under its own contradictions.

3. The Silent Embargo: The Supply Chain War

While the legal battle is noisy, the logistical war is silent.

Rebuilding the oil industry requires phenomenal quantities of equipment. The Americans supply the high technology, but the steel, standard valves, and cables come from China.

The "Houston Plan" had planned to purchase these cheap materials from Asia. But starting in mid-February 2026:

- **Burton & Hall** 's subcontractors are accepted but never delivered.
- Chinese banks are blocking SWIFT transfers due to "suspicion of money laundering".
- China imposes a strict quota on the export of rare earth elements to Latin America.

In Caracas, American engineers are tearing their hair out. They have to turn to German or Japanese suppliers, 40% more expensive. The reconstruction budget is exploding.

4. The Financial "Trojan Horse": Private Debt

China is playing one last vicious card.

Many American hedge funds *hold* Venezuelan debt. By declaring the debt "odious," Washington also threatens the interests of these American investors.

In private rooms in Hong Kong, emissaries from the **Beijing Sovereign Fund** (Chinese sovereign wealth fund) are proposing an alliance to American hedge funds:

- *"Washington wants to erase us. Let's join forces legally. We will finance your lawsuits in New York against debt cancellation."*

Law firms like **Gibson Law** , indirectly paid by Beijing, are beginning to file appeals challenging the constitutionality of the debt cancellation. Washington finds itself under attack from within, from its own financial system.

5. Operation "Digital Vault": The End of SWIFT

Faced with the stalemate, the US Treasury Secretary decides to change the rules of the monetary game.

On March 5, 2026, the US administration created the **Venezuela Reconstruction Special Purpose Vehicle (VR-SPV)** .

It's not a bank. It's a large digital ledger hosted directly on the **Federal Reserve 's servers** .

The system operates in a closed circuit:

1. **Purchase : Alamo Refining** buys Venezuelan oil. It credits the VR-SPV account at the Fed.
2. **Storage:** The money remains with the Fed, protected by absolute sovereign immunity. No European or Asian judge can seize it.
3. **Payment:** The Fed pays **Burton & Hall** or **AmeriCorp directly** .

The money never leaves American soil. Venezuela no longer has monetary sovereignty.

Tokenization (RingPay & CoinBaseX)

To pay local wages, the USA is launching the **"Libertad Dollar"** , a *stablecoin* developed in partnership with **RingPay** and **CoinBaseX** .

Workers receive digital tokens through an app. China cannot seize these funds. Venezuela is becoming a testing ground for the digital dollar, impervious to sanctions.

6. The Technological Graveyard: Planned Obsolescence

In retaliation, China activates the **"Logistics Kill Switch"** .

Venezuela had been equipped with Chinese technology.

- Trains? **China Rail** Corp.
- Telecoms? **H-Tech** and **Z-Com** .
- The buses? **Tong Motors** .
- The dams? **HydroChina** .

In mid-March 2026, 4G networks collapse. **H-Tech routers** stop receiving updates. **China Rail Corp locomotives** break down due to a lack of parts. American engineers from **Syscom** and **American Bell** attempt to replace the network, but it's too slow. The Venezuelan economy grinds to a halt.

7. The War of the "Vultures": Betrayal on Wall Street

On April 12, 2026, a consortium of American funds led by **Onyx Capital** (BlackRock), supported by Chinese evidence, sues the US government before the Supreme Court.

Argument: *"By creating a closed financial circuit at the Fed to favor **AmeriCorp** and deprive other creditors, the government is violating property rights."*

Washington panics and invokes "National Security" to prohibit the examination of the accounts. The moral legitimacy of the intervention crumbles on Wall Street.

8. The Zurich Pact: The Secret Partition

At the end of May 2026, the situation is at a standstill. A secret meeting takes place in Zurich between Americans and Chinese. No Venezuelans are present.

A cynical compromise, the "Grand Bargain", is signed:

1. **North for America (Hydrocarbons):** China ceases legal harassment of tankers. It *de facto recognizes* the primacy of US companies (**Titan** , **AmeriCorp**) in the oil fields.
2. **The South for China (Minerals):** In exchange, the USA allows China to regain exclusive control of the **Orinoco Mining Arc** (south of the river).
    - Chinese companies **China Trust** and **AluChina** obtain perpetual concessions for gold and coltan.
    - This is how the "odious" debt will be repaid: in kind, through the plundering of the South's mineral resources.

The Consequence: The Country Divided in Two

Venezuela is partitioned.

- To the North: A "Dollar" zone, under American protection, Miami culture, **Sentinel Global security** .
- To the South: A "Yuan" zone, under Chinese influence, **H-Tech technology** , mining worker camps.

The Venezuelan state is now nothing more than a buffer.

The US saved its oil supply, but at the cost of militarizing the Dollar and ceding half the country to its strategic rival.

Meanwhile, in Midland, Texas, independent oil producers are beginning to realize that the massive influx of Venezuelan crude is killing their own businesses. The crisis is spreading inland.

A. The Ghost of Rotterdam: The Seizure of the Century

Port of Rotterdam, Europoort Terminal. February 5, 2026. 06:00.

Norwegian captain Lars Jansen drank his black coffee as he watched the tugboats approach the immense hull of his ship, the *Titan Sovereign* .

It was a monster, 330 meters long, a VLCC (*Very Large Crude Carrier*) loaded to the brim with 2 million barrels of *Merey 16 crude oil* extracted three weeks earlier in Venezuela by **Titan Energy** .

Cargo value: $140 million.

Destination: The Shell refinery in Pernis.

Jansen was relaxed. The Atlantic crossing had been uneventful. The weather was fine. In six hours, he would be ashore, ready to take a train to Amsterdam and enjoy a three-day leave.

The radio crackled.

— *Titan Sovereign* , this is Rotterdam Port Control. Please stop the engines immediately. Do not take the mooring lines.

Jansen frowned.

— Control, this is Jansen. We are in the approach channel. It's dangerous to stop here. What's the problem?

— You're expecting visitors, Captain. Keep the canal open.

Jansen looked out the porthole. It wasn't customs. A Dutch Port Police speedboat, escorted by a black civilian vessel, was speeding toward them.

Ten minutes later, six men boarded the gangway. Four armed police officers and two civilians in gray suits, uncomfortable in their orange life jackets. One of the civilians handed Jansen a laminated folder.

"Captain, I am Mr. Van Der Hout. I represent **SinoOil** and the **Bank of Beijing Development** . Here is a *Mareva Injunction* , issued by the Rotterdam Commercial Court an hour ago.

" "A seizure?" Jansen barked . "This oil belongs to **Titan Energy** , an American company!"

"Not anymore," the lawyer replied calmly. "According to the summary judgment, this oil was illegally extracted from a concession belonging to **SinoOil** , which was expropriated without compensation by the de facto Venezuelan government. This oil is stolen property."

Jansen looked at the document. It had official stamps, judges' signatures.

— And my ship?

Your vessel is under judicial seizure until ownership of the cargo is established. This could take... six months. Sorry for your permission to leave Amsterdam, Captain.

Titan HQ in Houston. He knew what was going to happen.

The second this news reached Bloomberg terminals, marine insurance prices would skyrocket. China had just turned Venezuelan oil into legal poison. No one in Europe would dare buy it anymore. The legal blockade had begun.

B. The Broken Chain: "Sorry, out of stock"

Burton & Hall headquarters, Houston, Texas. February 20, 2026.

Sarah Miller, Vice President of *Supply Chain* , hadn't slept for 48 hours. Her office resembled a war room. Screens displayed the location of hundreds of containers around the world.

All the warning lights were flashing RED.

The Venezuela reconstruction project consumed astronomical quantities of materials. To meet deadlines and stay within budget, **Burton & Hall** had relied entirely on Chinese suppliers, who were cheaper and faster.

But for the past week, the machine had been jammed.

Sarah screamed into her telephone headset.

— What do you mean "stuck in Shanghai"? The container of high-pressure valves was supposed to leave on Tuesday!

At the other end of the line, his liaison officer in Shanghai, an American expatriate, had a trembling voice.

— Sarah, it's blocked. Chinese customs introduced a new procedure this morning: "Enhanced Environmental Compliance Inspection" for all industrial equipment destined for Latin America.

— That's nonsense! These valves are up to standard!

— I know. But they're inspecting each valve one by one. By hand. They say it's going to take three months.

"Three months? But I have teams in Venezuela waiting for this equipment to seal a leaking well! If I don't get these valves, the well will explode!"

She hung up abruptly. She turned to her deputy.

"Find me an alternative." "We've looked," said the deputy, exhausted. "There's a supplier in Germany, *Siemens* .

" "How much?" "Forty percent more expensive. And the delivery time is six months. Their order book is full." "And in Japan?" "Same thing. Everyone depends on Chinese steel. Sarah... we're stuck. We can't rebuild Venezuela without China. They control the supply of spare parts."

Sarah slumped into her chair. She realized the magnitude of the strategic error. The United States had sent soldiers and lawyers. China had simply stopped sending bolts. And China was winning.

"Call the State Department," she whispered. "Tell them the project's budget just doubled. And tell them it's their fault."

C. The Hong Kong Pact: The Enemy of My Enemy

Private club "The China Club", Hong Kong. March 2, 2026.

The atmosphere was hushed, scented with jasmine tea and Cuban cigars.

At a secluded table sat two men who represented two opposing worlds. On one side was **Marcus Thorn** , manager of an ultra-aggressive New York *hedge fund* (**Apex Management**). He wore a $5,000 suit and had a reputation for gutting companies for breakfast. He held $2 billion in Venezuelan bonds, which had become worthless since Washington had declared the debt "odious." He was furious.

On the other side was **Mr. Li** , a discreet emissary of the **Beijing Sovereign Fund** . He wore an unbranded suit and drank hot water.

"Mr. Thorn," Li began in perfect English. "We have a common problem. Washington is stealing from us."

"Washington is trying to 'restructure for democracy,'" Thorn corrected cynically. "But yes, they're stealing my 2 billion. They've decided Maduro's debt doesn't count. It's communism disguised as freedom." "Ironical, isn't it?" Li smiled . "Communist China defends property rights, and capitalist America abolishes them."

He placed a small USB key on the table.

— You want to sue the American government, Mr. Thorn. You want to go to the Supreme Court to have this debt cancellation overturned. But lawyers are expensive.

"I have the means," Thorn grumbled.

Why spend your money? We're ready to finance your legal fees. In full. Through shell companies in the Cayman Islands. No one will know it's Chinese money.

Thorn looked at the USB key.

— What's on it?

PetroVen emails , signed contracts, proof that the money loaned by China and by you was indeed used to build infrastructure, and not to buy weapons as Washington claims. This is the ammunition you need to win your case.

Thorn took the USB drive. He knew he was making a deal with the devil. He was going to use the money and intelligence of America's strategic rival to humiliate his own government.

But Marcus Thorn wasn't a patriot. He was a capitalist.

"What do you want in return?" Thorn asked.

"Nothing. Just that you win. If you win, the legal precedent is broken. And we get our money back too. The enemy of my enemy is my banker.

" Thorn shook Li's hand.

— Deal done. We're going to give them a hell of a lawsuit.

D. The Fed Bunker: Coding the Fortress

Basement of the Federal Reserve Bank of New York, Manhattan. March 10, 2026.

While China attacked on the legal and logistical front, America prepared its technological counter-attack.

The room didn't look like a bank. It looked like a Silicon Valley start-up, but with armed guards at the entrance.

A team of thirty coders, recruited by the NSA and **CoinBaseX** , worked day and night.

David, the project manager, projected the diagram onto the giant screen in front of the Secretary of the Treasury who had come to inspect the work.

— Mr. Secretary, here is **Project V-Account** .

The diagram showed a closed circle.

"The current problem," David explained, "is that as soon as oil money touches a commercial bank (JP Morgan, Citi), it becomes vulnerable to seizure by the Chinese or Europeans. The SWIFT system has become a battleground."

"The solution?" asked the Secretary.

— We are leaving the banking system. We have created a private "Ledger" (ledger), hosted here, on the Fed's servers.

David clicked.

— When **AmeriCorp** buys oil, they don't transfer dollars. They transfer digital "Tokens" to this ledger. These tokens are only redeemable here.

— And how do they pay the workers in Venezuela?

— This is phase 2. The **RingPay app** . Every Venezuelan receives a digital wallet on their phone. They're given "Libertad Coins." They can use them to pay for bread. China can't block this because it doesn't go through any correspondent bank. It goes through the NSA's cloud.

The Treasury Secretary looked at the screen. It was bright. And terrifying.

"Are you telling me we're creating a parallel currency?" "We're creating a militarized dollar, sir. Unreachable. Invisible. It's the only way to circumvent the Chinese legal blockade."

"Do it," ordered the Secretary. "But if it fails and the Venezuelan economy collapses, it's your fault."

E. The "Blackout": The Huawei Switch

Digitel Network Control Center, Caracas. March 15, 2026.

China's response to the invention of the digital dollar was swift. It was brutal and physical.

Venezuela, under Chávez, had entrusted all of its telecom infrastructure to China (**H-Tech** and **Z-Com**).

Pedro, a Venezuelan network engineer, was watching his monitoring screens. Everything was green. Suddenly, at precisely 2:00 PM, a command arrived.

It didn't come from her keyboard. It came from a remote server, located in Shenzhen. The command was: *SYS_HALT_CRITICAL_UPDATE* .

"What's going on?" shouted his colleague.

— The routers are restarting! All of them!

— They're doing an update in the middle of the day?

The screens went black. Then they came back on with an error message: *LICENSE EXPIRED. CONTACT VENDOR.*

"Expired license? " Pedro stammered . "But we paid!"

"No," said the colleague, looking at his phone. "We've lost all signal. No 4G. No fiber."

Across the country, digital silence fell.

The payment terminals went dark.

The **RingPay app** , which Washington relied on to pay people, became unusable. Without the internet, cryptocurrency doesn't exist.

US military communications switched to their backup satellite networks, but for the civilian economy, it was brain death.

In Beijing, a civil servant closed his laptop. He had just proven a theory: *"You control the money? We control the cables. Try spending your digital dollar without the internet."*

America had built a financial fortress, but China had just cut electricity .

CHAPTER 5: THE TEXAS DILEMMA AND THE POLITICAL TRAP

When Venezuelan black gold kills the American shale miracle.

Midland, Texas (Permian Basin). April 15, 2026.

The Midland *Petroleum Club* is nothing like the plush lounges of Zurich or Manhattan. Here, the steaks are bigger, the voices are louder, and ostrich-skin boots aren't a fashion accessory, but a work tool. This is the epicenter of the *Shale Revolution* , the place that made the United States the world's leading oil power.

Usually, at this time of year, the parking lot is full of brand-new Ford F-250s, bought outright with year-end bonuses. But this afternoon, the atmosphere is somber. At the bar, Jim "Big Dog" Reynolds, owner of an independent drilling company (*Wildcatter*), is watching **WNN** (World News Network) on the giant screen.

The news ticker scrolls: *"RECORD: Venezuelan oil imports reach 1.5 million barrels/day. Gasoline prices at the pump drop by 15 cents."*

Jim stubbed out his cigar in a rage.

"Look at those traitors in Washington. We voted for them. We supported the invasion. We thought they were going to kick out the communists so we could sell our technology there. And what are they doing? They're flooding the market with that cheap socialist garbage and killing us. Every barrel that comes in from Caracas is one less barrel I can sell in Houston."

This very morning, Jim had to lay off two drilling crews and shut down three wells in Reeves County. His bank called him: with the drop in the price of West Texas Intermediate (WTI) crude caused by refinery saturation, his margins had turned negative.

This is the stark paradox of Operation *Absolute Resolve* . It was sold to Texans as an American victory. But in economic reality, it is becoming the worst nightmare of independent American producers. Venezuelan oil is not supplementing Texas oil; it is driving it out.

1. The Oil Civil War: *Upstream* vs. *Downstream*

To understand the simmering anger in the red (Republican) states, one must dissect the schizophrenia of the American oil industry. The general public sees "Big Oil" as a single bloc. This is false. There are two camps with diametrically opposed interests.

The Winners' Camp: The Refiners (*Downstream*)

These are the giants: **Alamo Refining** , **Spartan Downstream** , **Route 66 Energy** , and the refining divisions of **Titan Energy** and **AmeriCorp** .

Their business model is simple: buy crude oil as cheaply as possible, refine it, and sell the gasoline as expensively as possible.

For them, returning from Venezuela is a divine blessing.

- They buy Venezuelan heavy crude (Merey) at a massive discount (at $50 a barrel).
- They are running their factories at full capacity.
- Their profit margins are exploding. They are the main beneficiaries of the "Houston Plan".

The Losers' Camp: Independent Producers (*Upstream*)

These are the thousands of small and medium-sized enterprises (SMEs) in Texas, North Dakota, and Oklahoma. Companies like **Frontier Shale** , **Eagle Rock Resources** , or **Rattlesnake Energy** .

Their model is the reverse: they extract (light) shale oil and need the price of crude to be high (above $70) to make their expensive drilling (hydraulic fracturing) profitable.

For them, Venezuela is poison.

- The massive influx of Venezuelan oil is saturating the storage capacity of the Gulf of Mexico.
- Refiners, saturated with heavy crude, are buying less light

Texan crude.

- As a result, the price of *WTI Midland* (the local crude) collapsed. On April 10, 2026, it fell below $60, the breakeven price *for* most small drilling companies.

This is a fratricidal war. The Trump Administration finds itself in an impossible position: it has satisfied the refiners, but it has stabbed its most loyal electoral base in the back: the small bosses of Texas oil.

2. The Mechanism of Exclusion: The "Wall of Mixing"

The technical argument put forward by the White House was: *"Venezuelan oil (heavy) and Texan oil (light) are complementary."*

It was a lie by omission.

Logistics Saturation

The pipelines running from the Permian Basin to the coast are full. But the problem lies at the end of the pipeline, in Corpus Christi and Houston.

The storage terminals are congested with Venezuelan crude arriving on supertankers. Refiners like **Alamo Refining** favor Venezuelan crude because it offers better profit margins.

The physical consequence: Texas crude no longer has an immediate market. It's accumulating in tanks in Midland.

The Effect of the "Recipe"

American refineries operate like kitchens.

Before 2026, due to a lack of heavy crude, they used a degraded recipe: a lot of light Texan crude mixed with imported residues.

Now that they have access to "pure" Venezuelan heavy crude, they are returning to their ideal recipe from the 90s: 70% heavy, 30% light.

This means they mechanically need **less** shale oil.

Domestic demand for **Frontier Shale oil** fell by 15% in three months. For the Texas economy, this is an instant recession.

3. The Donors' Revolt: Ultimatum to Washington

The anger is not confined to the bars of Midland. It is rising in Washington DC, transported by the private jets of Republican donors.

Trump International Hotel, Washington DC. April 20, 2026.

A crisis meeting is being held in a private suite.

On one side, the White House chief of staff.

On the other side, there are the bosses of **Rattlesnake Energy** and **Frontier Shale** . These men are worth billions of dollars and finance the Super-PACs that get conservative senators elected.

The tone is not diplomatic:

"Mr. Secretary, you lied to us. You handed over the American market to ***AmeriCorp*** *and* ***Titan*** *. "*

My guys in North Dakota are going bankrupt.

Here's the reality: if you don't block or tax this Venezuelan oil within a month, we'll cut off funding for the November midterm elections.

This is a political nuclear threat. The Republican Party cannot afford to lose Texas or Oklahoma.

4. The "Solution": The Return of the SPR

In an attempt to quell the rebellion, the White House is improvising.

On May 1, 2026, the Department of Energy announced a **"Strategic Security Initiative"** .

The idea is to artificially manipulate demand to support Texas crude prices.

The federal government is committed to massively purchasing American light crude to fill the **Strategic Petroleum Reserve** (SPR).

- **The Deal:** The state buys 100 million barrels from independent producers at a guaranteed floor price of $70.
- **The Financing:** To pay these 7 billion dollars, the State uses the revenues... from royalties of Venezuelan oil (via the Fed's VR-SPV account described in Chapter 4).

It's a circular gas plant: Venezuelan oil money (which is killing the Texas market) is used to subsidize Texas producers (so they don't die).

5. Exporting the Crisis: Transatlantic Blackmail

But internal bailouts are not enough. The physical surplus of oil must be disposed of.

Washington decides to implement the **"Great Spill" strategy** . Since America cannot consume its own oil (because it consumes Venezuelan oil), it must force the rest of the world to consume American oil.

NATO Headquarters, Brussels, Belgium. May 25, 2026.

The US Secretary of Commerce projects a stark graphic in front of European ambassadors.

"Ladies and gentlemen, the United States guarantees your military security. This security comes at a cost. Our producers are suffering because we have secured Venezuela for the good of the Free World."

It's time for Europe to pay its share. By July 1st, we expect the European Union to replace 40% of its current imports with American light crude oil and Texas liquefied natural gas (LNG).

The German representative attempts to raise an objection regarding the price. The American response is scathing:

"That's the price of freedom, Hans. If you prefer to buy your energy elsewhere, perhaps you should also look for your nuclear umbrella elsewhere."

6. The "Freedom Energy Act": Socialism for the Rich

In Washington, Congress urgently passes the **"Freedom Energy Act"** .

Under the guise of "national security", this law establishes a tax credit mechanism.

- **The principle:** For each barrel exported to an "allied country", the producer receives a federal tax credit of $5.
- **The effect:** This allows Texas producers to sell their oil to

Europe *below their production cost* (dumping), while remaining profitable thanks to the subsidy.

The circle is complete:

1. The US is taking oil from Venezuela.
2. The profits from this oil are used to subsidize Texas oil.
3. This subsidized Texan oil is being dumped in Europe.

In June 2026, at the G7 summit in Miami, the European Union signs the **Transatlantic Energy Partnership Pact** . Europe commits to massive purchases of American gas and oil, sealing its total energy dependence.

In the streets of Berlin and Paris, protests erupt against the "Texas Tax." The transatlantic alliance holds militarily, but is rotting socially.

7. The Asian Front and Green Hypocrisy

Japan and South Korea, terrified by China, are also being urged to buy American. Convoys of **Spartan Downstream LNG carriers** are leaving Louisiana for Tokyo.

The darkest aspect is environmental. To enable this export frenzy, the Administration has dismantled environmental protections. In the Permian Basin, methane leaks are ignored by the EPA.

The official narrative rebrands American gas as **"Clean Freedom Molecules** . "

The energy lobby funds studies via **Massachusetts Strategy Group** (BCG) explaining that American gas is "greener" thanks to dubious carbon offsets purchased... in southern Venezuela, in the Chinese mining region (see Chapter 4).

8. The Political Payoff: The November 2026 Elections

We are approaching the fall of 2026. The midterm elections are near.

Six months ago, the Republican Party was in jeopardy. Today, a miracle has occurred.

- In Midland, the **Frontier Shale wells** are drilling again.
- **Alamo** refineries are running at full capacity thanks to Venezuelan oil.
- **Titan Energy** and **AmeriCorp** 's profits are breaking records.

The President holds his campaign rallies in front of working oil derricks:

"They said we couldn't do it! We secured our borders, we secured our energy, and we brought Europe and China to heel. America has once again become the World's Powerhouse!"

The crowd erupts in jubilation. The Texan voter doesn't care about the cost of heating in Berlin. The Republicans retain Texas and strengthen their majority in the Senate.

A. The Silence of the Donkeys: The Bankruptcy of Midland

Reeves County, West Texas. May 10, 2026.

The most terrifying sound for a Texas oilman isn't an explosion. It's silence.

Jim "Big Dog" Reynolds stood, his ostrich-skin boots covered in red dust, in front of his *Liberty-4 well* .

In front of him, the lead horse (the "Nodding Donkey", the rocker pump) was motionless. The engine was cold.

"Why did you arrest him, Earl?" Jim asked his foreman.

"The tanks are full, Boss," Earl replied, spitting out tobacco. "The **Sunoco truck** didn't come this morning. They say the terminals at Cushing are saturated. They're not taking a drop of light crude anymore."

Jim took out his phone. He called his broker in Houston.

— Eddy, what the hell is going on? I have 5,000 barrels sitting here.

— I'm sorry, Jim. It's a bloodbath. **Alamo Refining** has cancelled all its spot purchase contracts for Texas crude.

- For what ?

They received three supertankers of Venezuelan heavy crude this morning. They're filling their storage facilities to capacity. They no longer need our light crude for their blends. WTI Midland is trading at $58 a barrel. Your break-even point is $65, Jim. If you sell, you lose money.

Jim hung up. He looked at the horizon. Hundreds of pumps lay idle across the plain.

A black car was approaching. It was the regional bank's car. Jim knew what was coming. He had put his house and ranch up as collateral to finance this drilling. "We won the war, Earl," Jim murmured. "The Marines took Caracas. And to thank us, Washington sends us the bill. **Titan Energy** and **AmeriCorp** are gorging themselves on Maduro's oil, and we, the small independents who brought energy independence to this country, are being asked to die in silence."

The bank employee got out of the car with a file under his arm.

— Mr. Reynolds, we need to talk about your deadlines.

Jim placed his hand on the butt of his revolver at his belt, an old reflex, then withdrew it. This wasn't the Wild West. This was Wall Street. You didn't shoot a banker. "Earl, lock down the site. We're bankrupt."

B. Suite 404: The Donors' Plot

Trump International Hotel, Washington DC. May 20, 2026.

Midland's anger had reached the capital.

In suite 404, the air was thick with cigar smoke and threats. The Oklahoma Senator (Chairman of the Energy Commission) was facing three men in Italian suits. They represented the **DEPA** (*Domestic Energy Producers Alliance*), the lobby for independent producers. Among them was the CEO of **Frontier Shale** .

— Senator, the CEO began without preamble, have you seen the employment figures in Texas? 15,000 fewer jobs in two months.

"I know, Bill, I know. It's an adjustment period..." "Adjustment my ass!" yelled the CEO. "It's premeditated murder."

The administration opened the floodgates of Venezuelan oil to appease the refiners of **Alamo** and the voters on the East Coast who want cheap gasoline. But you've forgotten who's funding your campaigns.

He placed an iPad on the table. It displayed a graph of campaign donations. "Next month is the Midterm fundraiser. **Frontier Shale** , **Rattlesnake Energy** , and **Eagle Rock** plan to donate $50 million to the Republican Super PAC."

The Senator smiled nervously.

— We are counting on your support, as always.

"You misunderstood me, Senator. This money is frozen. Worse: if you don't find a market for our oil by June 1st, we'll give that money to your primary opponents. We'll fund radical 'America First' candidates who will campaign on the theme 'Washington betrayed Texas.' We're going to destroy you politically."

The Senator paled. Losing the support of the independent oil companies meant certain political death.

— What do you want? A tax on Venezuelan oil?

"Impossible," said the CEO. "The President promised cheap gasoline. He won't tax imports."

— So what?

— We don't care about cheap gas in the US. We want a market. If we can't sell our oil here because the refineries are full of Venezuelan crude, then find us someone else to sell it to. — Who? China isn't buying anymore (see Chapter 4).

"Europe," said the CEO. "Force the Europeans to buy our shale. They're rich, they're compliant. Make them pay top dollar. Figure it out yourselves. But empty our tanks."

C. The Brussels Ambush: Colt Diplomacy

NATO Headquarters, Brussels. May 25, 2026. 10:00 a.m.

The meeting was not on the official agenda. It took place in a secure "SCIF" room in the basement.

The US Secretary of Commerce, special envoy of the White House, was facing the Ambassadors of Germany, France and Italy.

There were no biscuits, no water. Just an electrical current.

"Gentlemen," the American began. "The situation in Ukraine is stable, but precarious. The American Congress is questioning the wisdom of maintaining 40,000 US troops in Europe if our partners do not play their part in economic solidarity."

The French ambassador adjusted his glasses.

"Mr. Secretary, we are meeting our NATO commitments of 2% of GDP." "That's good. But we're talking about energy security. America made a huge sacrifice in liberating Venezuela. That destabilized our domestic market. We have a surplus of light crude oil and natural gas (LNG)."

He signaled to his aide, who distributed a document entitled **"Transatlantic Energy Partnership Pact** . "

The German ambassador scanned the document. His eyes widened.

"Is this a joke? You're asking Germany to commit to fixed purchase volumes of American LNG for 10 years? At a price indexed to the US market plus 20%? But that's 30% more expensive than Qatari gas!" "Qatari gas doesn't come with a nuclear umbrella," the American replied coldly. "And what about oil?" added the Italian. "Our refineries aren't configured for Texas light crude. We'd have to invest billions to adapt our plants!"

"Then invest," the American declared. "It's that or..."

He left the sentence hanging.

— Or what?

Or the President could reconsider his position on Article 5 at the next summit. He might consider that defending Europe is too heavy a burden for a struggling American economy.

A deathly silence fell over the room. It was protection racket, pure and simple. Like the mafia selling fire insurance.

"You are asking us to save your Texas producers from bankruptcy," the Frenchman summarized bitterly.

"I'm offering you energy freedom," the American corrected with a predatory smile. "You have until June 1st to sign. Otherwise, **Frontier Shale** will go bankrupt, and the next American president will be an isolationist who will withdraw troops from Germany. The choice is yours."

D. The Laboratory of Lies: "Green Freedom"

Massachusetts Strategy Group (BCG) offices, Boston. June 2, 2026.

Once Europe was twisted, the pill had to be sold to the public.

American shale oil and LNG had a disastrous image in Europe: pollution, fracking, methane. The German Greens were going to howl. Oil had to be repainted green.

In the creativity room of the consulting firm, a team of bright and cynical young communicators were brainstorming.

"The problem," said the project manager, "is that Texas LNG has a disgusting carbon footprint. Between extraction, liquefaction, and transportation, it's worse than coal."

"You can't change the chemistry," said one analyst.

"No, but we can change the accounting," replied the director.

He wrote on the whiteboard: **OFFSET (Compensations)**.

— We're going to create a certificate. We'll call it... "Certified Responsible Natural Gas".

— On what basis?

carbon credits .

— Where? In Europe, it's too expensive.

"In Venezuela!" exclaimed the director. "That's the perfect irony. The southern part of Venezuela, the part controlled by the Chinese (see Chapter 4), is a jungle. We buy 'non-deforestation' credits from the Chinese for next to nothing. We slap this certificate on Texas gas. And boom! The gas becomes 'carbon neutral.'"

"Wait," said the analyst. "We're paying the Chinese to greenwash the American gas we're forcing

Europeans to buy?

— Exactly. That's globalization.

— The environmentalists will kill us if they find out.

They won't learn it. The calculation is too complex. We'll make a great ad with a wind turbine and an LNG tanker at sunset. Slogan: *"Molecules of US Freedom - Clean Power for a Safe World* . "

Thus was sealed the ecological scam of the century. Dirty shale gas from Texas became, through the magic of a PowerPoint presentation in Boston, the cornerstone of the European energy transition.

E. The Corpus Christi Terminal: The Traffic Jam

Port of Corpus Christi, Texas. June 15, 2026.

Jim "Big Dog" Reynolds had returned from hell.

He was standing on the deck of a pleasure boat, looking out at the harbor channel. It was a massive traffic jam.

Dozens of supertankers were waiting their turn to load. They weren't coming from Venezuela. They were heading to Rotterdam, Le Havre, and Tokyo.

His phone rang. It was Earl, his foreman.

— Boss, we received the order from **Frontier Shale** . We're restarting the pumps.

— At what price?

— $72 per barrel.

Jim smiled. The plan had worked. The federal government, through the *Freedom Energy Act* , subsidized each barrel exported by $5 (paid with money stolen from Venezuela), and the Europeans bought it all at high prices under threat.

"Earl, hire two more crews. We'll drill day and night. Europe is thirsty."

Jim looked at the ships. He saw a giant LNG carrier, the *Spirit of Texas* . On its hull, a freshly painted green banner: *"Net-Zero Cargo* . "

Jim burst out laughing. He lit a cigar.

"God bless America," he said. "And God bless creative accountants."

F. The Submission of Tokyo: Bitter Tea

Prime Minister's Residence, Tokyo, Japan. June 20, 2026.

While Europe had protested, Japan had submitted in dignified but painful silence.

The American Ambassador was drinking tea with the Minister of Economy, Trade and Industry (METI). "Your Excellency," said the Japanese Minister, "our refiners **ENEOS** and **Idemitsu** are very concerned. American light crude is highly volatile. There are safety risks at our older facilities."

"I understand," said the Ambassador. "But you know what's more volatile? The South China Sea."

The Japanese Minister lowered his eyes.

"The Seventh Fleet needs fuel to patrol," the American continued. "And the American economy needs to sell that fuel. It's a virtuous cycle. If you buy our oil, you're paying for your own protection." "We will reduce our purchases from Saudi Arabia," the Minister conceded. "Wise decision. The Saudis are no longer reliable. They talk too much to the Chinese. America is your only friend. But friendship has a market price."

The Ambassador put down his cup.

— Oh, one last thing. We have a surplus of genetically modified corn in Iowa. **Midwest Grain** is looking for outlets. I'm sure the Japanese market would be delighted to open its quotas, wouldn't it?

The Japanese Minister swallowed hard. He understood that this was only the beginning. Venezuela had whetted the appetite of the American behemoth. Now that they had tasted "forced trade," they were going to apply it to everything: oil, gas, corn, beef. Japan, a loyal ally, had become a captive customer.

G. The Other Side of the Coin: Imported Inflation

Walmart Supermarket, Cleveland Suburbs, Ohio. July 4, 2026.

While Texans celebrated, Brenda, a mother of three,
was looking at his receipt.
She didn't understand.

On TV, the President said that America had once again become an energy superpower. Yet, the price of his shopping cart had increased by 15%.

Why? Because in order to export all that oil and gas, the dollar had become very strong. Too strong.

American industrial exports (excluding energy) were collapsing. Factories in Ohio were closing because they could no longer sell their machines abroad with such a strong dollar.

And since the US imported everything else (clothing, electronics, toys) and supply chains were disrupted by the trade war with China (Chapter 4), prices rose.

Brenda looked at the price of gasoline. It had gone down a little, yes. But the price of meat, bread, and clothes had skyrocketed.

She put away her groceries. She saw a Midterm election poster: *"VOTE REPUBLICAN - AMERICAN PROSPERITY"*.

She tore down the poster.

America had saved the oil industry, but it was killing its middle class. The "Texas Dilemma" had been solved at Ohio's expense.

Conclusion

Chapter 5 concludes with a nighttime satellite image of the Western Hemisphere.

It shows two patches of incandescent light, vying for intensity. To the south are the flares of Venezuela, burning gas to extract heavy oil destined for American refineries.

In the North, the flares of the Permian Basin in Texas, which burn excess gas from shale wells destined for Europe.

The United States has resolved its internal dilemma. It has saved Texas. But now it stands alone. Europe silently despises it. China is fighting it economically.

The American Empire is at its energy peak, but it has never been so morally isolated.

And while all eyes are on the tankers, another threat is growing: systemic corruption in the reconstruction effort. Billions of dollars are disappearing into the pockets of intermediaries like **Bauchet Construction** and **Flux Engineering** . This is **"Disaster Capitalism"** in all its glory, which we will explore in Chapter 6.

CHAPTER 6: THE ECONOMY OF RECONSTRUCTION AND THE CONSTRUCTION VULTURES

Where we discover that it is more profitable to bill for a hospital than to build one, and how American money ended up financing gangs.

Tamanaco InterContinental Hotel, Caracas. September 15, 2026.

The bar at the Tamanaco Hotel has always been a barometer of Venezuela's upheavals. In the 1970s, oil tycoons were seen ordering *Blue Label whisky* there. During the Chávez years, revolutionaries in red shirts were seen negotiating bribes there.

In September 2026, the clientele has changed. The military fatigues of the special forces have disappeared, replaced by khaki trousers from the brand *5.11 Tactical* and blue polo shirts with logos.

These are the men of the "Big Three" of American construction: **Bauchet**

Construction , **Flux Engineering** and **K-Root & Brown** .

They don't carry weapons, but iPad Pros. They don't speak Spanish, and they don't care. They are there because the US Congress has released the first tranche of the *"Venezuela Recovery Fund"* : $50 billion to rebuild civilian infrastructure.

From the terrace, they look down at the city below. They don't see the suffering. They see billing lines. Caracas has become the new Baghdad of 2003, but with one major difference: this time, there is money guaranteed by oil.

1. The Invention of the "VRA": The Automated Teller Machine

To understand how billions of dollars can vanish without result

To see what's visible, you have to look at the administrative structure.

The American administration created a parallel entity: the **VRA (Venezuela Reconstruction Authority)**.

Based within the fortified compound of the U.S. Embassy, the VRA is a state within a state.

1. **Total Immunity:** Its employees and subcontractors enjoy diplomatic immunity.
2. **Emergency Decree:** The VRA is exempt from standard tendering procedures. It can award contracts directly to **Bauchet** or **Flux** without competition.
3. **Circular Financing:** The VRA draws its budget directly from the Fed's escrow account (the VR-SPV). It is Venezuelan oil money that pays American companies. Venezuela is paying a heavy price for its own invasion.

2. The Mechanics of the "Cost-Plus" Contract

The core of the business model lies in the type of contract used: the **Cost-Plus Fixed Fee**.

The company is reimbursed for all its actual costs (*Cost*), plus a guaranteed profit margin (*Plus*) of 15%.

This system is perverse: **the more you spend, the more you earn.**

If **K-Root & Brown** builds a school for $1 million, it makes a $150,000 profit. If it manages to make the school cost $10 million (by importing cement from Miami, housing its engineers at the Ritz), it makes a $1.5 million profit.

Inefficiency becomes the engine of profit.

- **The Screw Case:** A box of screws that costs $10 in Caracas is billed at $400 to the VRA. Why? Because it is purchased in the USA, transported by special **Global Express** (DHL) plane, and cleared through customs by a private agent. Each step is a "reimbursable cost."

- **Empty Trucks:** Convoys of trucks make empty round trips between the port and Caracas. The logistics company is paid per kilometer traveled, not per ton delivered.

3. The Cascading Subcontracting: Trickle-Down to Nothingness

The American giants (**Prime Contractors**) don't lay a single brick themselves. They do "Project Management".

Level 1: The "Prime" (Flux Engineering)

Receives $100 million to renovate the water system. Keeps $30 million for its expenses.

Level 2: The "Major Sub" (An international firm)

Receives 70 million. Takes 20 million for his security.

Level 3: The Screen Company

He receives 50 million. This is where local politics comes into play. The new oligarchs create ad hoc construction companies. The boss takes 30 million and transfers it to the Cayman Islands.

Level 4: Reality

With the remaining 20 million, unskilled workers are hired. The pipe is laid, but it leaks after three months. On paper, 100 million has been invested.

4. Case Study: The "Power Barges" Scandal

Electricity is the absolute priority. The Guri hydroelectric network is in ruins. The VRA is launching the

"Power Bridge" program .

Instead of repairing the dam, the VRA signs a $2 billion contract with a Florida company, **EnerCorps** , to lease floating generator barges.

Technical Absurdity:

These barges run on diesel. Since Venezuela no longer has functioning diesel refineries, VRA has to *import* American diesel (supplied by **Alamo Refining**) to power the barges.

Cost of kWh produced: $0.45 (compared to $0.02 for hydroelectricity).

It's a financial black hole, but a jackpot for **EnerCorps** . Six months later, an investigation will reveal that three of the invoiced barges never left the port of Jacksonville.

5. Humanitarian Aid as a Weapon of War (USAID and Agribusiness)

USAID arrives with a massive budget for food aid. But the aid is subject to the **"Buy American Act"** .

American agricultural products .

USAID is flooding the country with rice from Arkansas and corn from Iowa supplied by **AgriCorp** and **Midwest Grain** .

These free or subsidized products are killing local agriculture. Venezuelan farmers can't compete. In six months, Andean agriculture is devastated. Venezuela becomes addicted to American imports. Humanitarian aid is, in reality, an export subsidy for the American Midwest.

6. The "Green Zone" and the Consultants

The Las Mercedes district has become a bubble of indecent prosperity. It is where expatriates and consultants from **Kinsey & Partners** or **Massachusetts Strategy Group live** .

These consultants charge millions to produce PowerPoint presentations that justify the expenses.

Meanwhile, in Catia, the "Grand Western Hospital" (300 million contract) is a ghost.

The Tennessee company in charge of the project received the money, poured a concrete slab, then declared "Force Majeure" to walk away with the funds. The children use the slab as a soccer field. They call it *"The Gringo Slab* . "

7. The Pax Mafiosa: When Crime Becomes a Subcontractor

But the darkest aspect of reconstruction is not white-collar corruption. It's violent corruption.

Barrio San Vicente, Maracay. October 20, 2026.

To gain entry to the water station rehabilitation site, engineers from the American firm **Tetra Solutions** show their badges to kids armed with AR-15 assault rifles and equipped with **MotoComm walkie-talkies** .

These kids belong to the **Tren de Aragua** , the mega criminal organization.

By pouring billions of dollars into a country without the rule of law, the United States made the classic mistake: they believed that money would buy peace. In reality, the money bought ammunition for the gangs.

8. The "Vacuna" and the Whitewashing

From the moment construction began, gangs blanketed the territory.

The rule imposed on American subcontractors is simple: **10% of the total budget of the project** (the *Vacuna*).

In exchange, the gang guarantees the safety of equipment and personnel.

How can a publicly traded company like **Flux Engineering** pay a gang?

Through shell companies.

1. The Gang creates a "Local Security" company.
2. The American company signs an official contract for "Perimeter Surveillance".
3. The invoices are audited by the VRA as legitimate expenses.

9. Case Study: The Eastern Gas Pipeline

The most blatant example is the rehabilitation of the *Anaco-Puerto Ordaz gas pipeline* by the Texas company **Texas Transfer** .

Initially, they hired an American private military company, **Sentinel Global** . The result: open warfare, exchanges of fire every night, construction site blocked.

In June 2026, **Texas Transfer** changed its strategy. They fired **Sentinel Global** and struck a deal with the area's "Boss," a local gang leader.

They paid $500,000 a month to his front company for security. The very next day, the shooting stopped. Construction progressed at record speed. American taxpayer money had been used to finance and arm a private militia that now controlled the region.

10. The Technology Theft and the War of Hearts

The gangs use this money for social programs. They distribute food and organize parties. In the neighborhoods, people say *"Thanks to the train* ." Organized crime is winning the battle for hearts and minds against an ineffective VRA (Republican Action Network).

More seriously, the Pentagon notes that high-tech equipment imported by **Bauchet** and **K-Root** is disappearing.

The **Aragua train** begins to use:

- Commercial drones to monitor the US Army.
- Encrypted communications from **OrbitalLink** (Starlink) were stolen.
- Reconstruction modernizes organized crime.

11. The Christmas Incident: The Kidnapping

On December 24, 2026, **Robert Miller** , deputy director of the VRA, is kidnapped in Caracas by a tactical commando using frequency jammers.

To secure his release, the United States must secretly negotiate and pay a ransom of $10 million in **Libertad Coins** (the cryptocurrency established by Washington).

Miller is freed, but the humiliation is complete. The incident proves that true power lies not in the embassy, but in Tocorón prison, the gang's headquarters.

A. The Lunch of Shame: Negotiating the "Vacuna"

Restaurant "La Estancia", Altamira district, Caracas. June 10, 2026.

It was a surreal scene that only Venezuela in 2026 could produce.

In this luxury grill, famous for its steaks, two men were having lunch at an isolated table at the back of the room.

The first was **Steve Bronson** , vice president of Latin American operations for **Flux Engineering** . He was wearing a grey Brooks Brothers suit, an ironed shirt, and was sweating profusely despite the air conditioning.

The second man called himself **"El Chino** ." He wore a red Adidas tracksuit, a baseball cap pulled low over his eyes, and a gold chain as thick as a finger. He didn't eat with cutlery, but speared pieces of meat with a tactical knife placed on the white tablecloth.

"Mr. Bronson," said El Chino, chewing loudly. "You have a fine project in Valencia. Refurbishment of the drinking water system. 80 million dollars, is that right?"

Bronson swallowed hard.

"It's a humanitarian project, Chino. It's for the people." "Of course. People need water. But people also need safety. And my boys in Valencia tell me your trucks are very fragile. A flat tire, an engine fire... it happens so fast."

"We hired **Sentinel Global** for security," Bronson retorted, trying to maintain a firm posture.

El Chino burst out laughing. A loud laugh that made the other tables turn around.

— **Sentinel** ? Those Colombian mercenaries? They don't know the terrain. They sleep in hotels. At night, the streets are ours. If you want your pipes to stay underground and not end up at the scrap yard, you have to pay for local insurance.

Bronson took out his handkerchief to mop his brow. He knew where this was leading. His CEO in Houston had told him: *"Do whatever it takes to get the project moving. We don't care about the details, we want to bill for the milestones."*

— How much? Bronson asked.

— 10%.

— That's impossible. I can't come up with 8 million in cash. VRA listeners will see that.

"Who's talking about cash?" said El Chino, pulling a crumpled piece of paper from his pocket. "You're going to sign a subcontract with this company: *'Servicios Logísticos Aragua SA* .' It's a legitimate company. You pay us for 'Community Relations Consulting' and 'Perimeter Surveillance.' You make a bank transfer every month. It's all above board. The VRA will stamp the invoice."

Bronson looked at the paper. He knew he was signing a pact with the devil. He was going to finance the **Aragua Railway** with American taxpayer money.

"If I sign, no more incidents?"

— Not a single one. Your trucks will be escorted by my motorcycles. Nobody will touch a bolt.

Bronson took out his pen.

— Okay. But I want the construction to be finished before Christmas.

— With us, Mr. Bronson, the trains always arrive on time. That's why we're called the *Tren* .

B. The Ghost of Catia: The Gringo's Plaque

Construction site of the Western General Hospital, Catia. August 14, 2026.

Dr. Sofia Mendez was walking through the mud. It had been raining for three days in Caracas, and the hospital construction site, meant to be the jewel of the reconstruction, resembled a swamp.

She was looking for the site manager from **Bauchet Construction**

.

She found him in an air-conditioned prefab building, playing cards on his computer.

"Where's the roof?" Sofia yelled. "You promised the emergency room roof would be installed in July! I have patients in tents in the courtyard, and they're getting wet!"

The American, a man named Hank, barely looked up.

— Calm down, Doctor. We're experiencing a delivery delay. The steel is held up in customs.

"That's not true!" she cried. "I saw the trucks arrive last week. And I saw them leave again at night! You sold the steel on the black market!"

Hank stood up. He was twice her size.

— Watch what you say, darling. That's slander. — I want to see the bills! I'm going to write to the SIGVR (Inspector General) in Washington!

Hank smiled. A contemptuous smile.

— Write to whomever you like. The Inspector is in Washington. I'm here. And here, I'm the one with the keys. Anyway, the budget's exhausted. — Exhausted? But you've only laid the foundations! Where did the 300 million go?

— Security costs, logistics, unforeseen geological issues... money goes fast, you know. We declared a case of force majeure this morning. We're stopping work on the site.

— Are you leaving?

— Demobilization. Order from headquarters.

Sofia emerged from the prefabricated building, trembling with rage.

She looked at the construction site. There was nothing there. Just concrete pillars sticking out of the ground like tombstones.

At the entrance to the site, there was one thing that was perfectly finished, shiny and clean: a large commemorative marble plaque.

It read in gold letters:

"Western General Hospital - Gift of the People of the United States of America to the Venezuelan People - Virtually Inaugurated by the President of the USA - 2026" .

Kids from the slum were already playing ball against the plate. Sofia sat down in the mud and cried. America had built a $50,000 plate and stolen a $300 million hospital.

C. The King of Tocorón: The True Center of Power

Tocorón Penitentiary Center, State of Aragua. September 2, 2026.

Tocorón was not a prison. It was a fortified city, a sovereign state off-limits to the police and the army for years.

Even after the invasion, the Americans had not dared to enter. They had surrounded the area, but left the interior to the "Prane" (the supreme leader), a man named **El Niño Guerrero** .

That evening, a black limousine with tinted windows approached the main gate of the prison. The corrupt Venezuelan National Guardsmen opened the gate.

The limousine entered *the* prison.

She stopped in front of the "Tokyo Disco," the private club built by the inmates inside the prison grounds. There were neon lights, loud reggaeton music, and a swimming pool.

A man emerged. He was not a prisoner. He was a CIA liaison officer, operating under diplomatic cover. He was carrying a briefcase.

El Niño Guerrero was waiting for him on a white leather sofa, surrounded by women and his lieutenants armed with gold-plated assault rifles.

"Welcome to my humble abode, Gringo," said Guerrero. "Would you like some whisky? I've got some 18-year-old."

"I'm in a hurry," said the CIA agent.

"Always in a hurry... That's why you're losing. So, what's the problem?" "The Eastern gas pipeline. The work is blocked by your men." "My men are hungry. Inflation, you know..."

"We've already paid for *Vacuna* ," said the agent.

— That was for the old rate. The price of cement has gone up. We need to renegotiate.

The officer placed the briefcase on the table.

— There are $2 million in **Libertad Coins** in these *cold wallets* (crypto keys). That's all we have. In exchange, I want the gas pipeline finished in a month. And I want you to hand over three Chavista "terrorists" so we can show them on TV and say we're making progress.

Guerrero laughed. He picked up a USB key.

— Okay for the gas pipeline. As for the terrorists... I'll find you three pathetic guys who no one will miss. You can put them in uniforms and say they were commanders.

— Deal concluded.

The CIA agent left. As he exited the prison, he passed a **Bauchet Construction delivery truck** pulling in. The truck was loaded with bricks and cement.

The materials, stolen from American construction sites, were being used to enlarge the gang leader's swimming pool. The American taxpayer was funding his worst enemy's hot tub. It was the perfect cycle of reconstruction.

D. Silent Night, Violent Night: The Abduction of Miller

Residential area of La Lagunita, Caracas. December 24, 2026. 11:45 PM.

Robert "Bob" Miller, the deputy director of the VRA, was a happy man. Christmas Eve at the Ambassador's had been perfect. He had drunk good wine, signed two big contracts with **K-Root & Brown** that would secure him a comfortable position on the board of directors once he returned home, and he was going back to his secure villa.

His convoy consisted of two armored Chevrolet Suburbans. Four **Sentinel Global guards** , former Navy SEALs, provided his protection. He felt untouchable.

"We're two minutes from the residence, Boss," the head of security said through his earpiece.

Suddenly, silence.

No radio. No GPS on the dashboard screen. No cell service. — *Jammer!* (Jammer!), yelled the guard. We're jammed!

At that very moment, a swarm of four drones appeared above the convoy. They were not military drones, but ultra-fast FPV racing drones, piloted with virtual reality headsets.

One of the drones crashed into the windshield of the lead vehicle. It exploded.

A shaped charge. The SUV's engine was completely destroyed.

The convoy stopped.

— Ambush! Left contact!

Shadows emerged from the bushes. They weren't shooting like amateurs. They were using blinding lasers to disorient the guards equipped with night-vision goggles.

It was a Special Forces level tactic.

The **Sentinel guards** fought back, but they were outnumbered.

A flashbang grenade exploded near Miller's door.

The door was torn off.

Miller found himself facing a hooded man wearing a tactical vest stolen from the US Army. " *Feliz Navidad, Mister Miller* ," the man said in English. "You're coming with us."

Miller was thrown into an unmarked van.

The operation lasted 90 seconds. No trace was left.

This was not a sordid kidnapping. It was a military operation carried out by the **Aragua Tren** , using technology (jammers, drones, night vision) that Miller himself had imported for reconstruction and which had been "lost" in the inventories.

The irony was complete: Miller had just been captured by his own budget.

E. Digital Ransom: Proof of Failure

VRA Bunker, American Embassy. December 26, 2026.

The video had arrived on a secure server.

Miller was seen there, sporting a black eye, holding a newspaper.

The kidnapper wasn't asking for cash. He was demanding a transfer of $15 million in **USDC-V** (the stablecoin).

And he provided a digital wallet address.

The CIA director in Caracas was watching the screen.

— Can we trace the wallet?

The cyber analyst shook his head.

— No, sir. They're using a Russian "Mixer" (crypto scrambler). And the final destination address... that's ironic.

- What ?

— It's a digital bank hosted in the Bahamas, an official partner of our **RingPay program** . They use our own financial infrastructure to launder the ransom.

The director slammed his fist on the table.

— Pay up. We can't let Miller get beheaded live on the internet. The President wouldn't take it well.

— Which budget line do we take the money from?

— Put it on the line "Unforeseen Technical Issues - Catia Hospital Project". Nobody will check there, it's just mud.

The transfer was completed in three clicks.

Miller was released the next day, thrown from a car in front of the Marriott Hotel. But the message had been received loud and clear by all American businesses: **The Boss isn't Uncle Sam. It's the Gang.**

From that day forward, the "Protection Tax" increased from 10% to 20%. And no one questioned it. The American occupation had become a cash cow for South American organized crime.

Conclusion

By January 2027, the "Reconstruction" program is a moral failure.

Of the $50 billion allocated, $40 billion has been spent, with only $5 billion of real value on the ground. The rest has been absorbed by the profit margins of American corporations and gang extortion.

"Disaster Capitalism" worked for shareholders and criminals. But by funding gangs to buy short-term social peace, the United States created monsters. These armed groups, now wealthy and equipped with drones, are beginning to engage in dialogue with former Chavista military personnel and laid-off engineers.

Reconstruction money has inadvertently funded the infrastructure for the future insurgency, which we will see erupt in **Chapter** 7 .

CHAPTER 7: THE HYBRID INSURRECTION AND THE SECURITY QUAG

The convergence of hatreds, the Salvadoran option, and the silent capitulation.

Orinoco Delta, Delta Amacuro State. April 19, 2027.

The mangrove is hell for a conventional army. It's a labyrinth of thousands of brackish waterways, tangled roots, and thick fog that renders the thermal cameras of *Predator drones* useless as soon as the sun sets. It is here, in this "Caribbean Vietnam," that America is losing control.

Staff Sergeant Miller of the *Green Berets* (Special Forces) observes the surface of the dark water from his river gunboat. His unit is tasked with securing the mouth of the river through which oil barges transit to the Atlantic. On paper, the region is pacified. CIA reports indicate that the "terrorist cells" were dismantled last year.

Suddenly, a deep drone drowns out the sound of the diesel engine. A swarm of fifty commercial drones—Chinese quadcopter models bought online—emerges from the canopy. They carry not cameras, but homemade C4 charges.

The swarm dives onto the gas compression station located on the shore, guarded by contractors from **Sentinel Global**.

The explosions are simultaneous. In ten seconds, three months' worth of gas production goes up in smoke.

This is not the work of angry peasants. It is a military strike. The enemy has mutated. This chapter recounts how, a year after the invasion, criminal gangs (financed by reconstruction), remnants of the Chavista army, and laid-off PetroVen technicians **formed** an unnatural alliance: the **"Mesa de Unidad Combatiente" (MUC)** . Their objective: to make a barrel of Venezuelan oil more expensive to steal than to buy.

1. The Holy Trinity of the Insurrection

For the Pentagon, Venezuela was a simple chessboard: the "Good Guys" (the transitional government) versus the "Bad Guys." But reality created a chimera.

In early 2027, a secret meeting was held in a suite at the Eurobuilding Hotel in Caracas. Three men sat there:

1. **The Prane (The Crime):** The head of the *Aragua Train* . He has the money (hundreds of millions diverted from reconstruction) and the workforce.
2. **The General (The Strategy):** A former military intelligence officer, on the run. He has tactical expertise.
3. **The Engineer (Technical):** A former **PetroVen executive** , purged by **AmeriCorp** . He knows every valve in the oil network.

The Devil's Pact: These groups hated each other, but the occupation brought them together. Their strategy is **"Profitable Sabotage"** .

2. Drone Warfare and Asymmetry

The insurgency is fighting with 3D printers and *open-source software* .

In clandestine workshops in Petare, engineers are modifying agricultural drones.

- **The Payload:** Shaped charges capable of piercing the hull of a crude oil tank.
- **Guidance:** Optical guidance by AI, insensitive to American GPS jamming (a technology ironically copied from software stolen from **Flux Engineering**).

For **Praetorian Group (the private security firm) and the US Army, life becomes a nightmare.** *Patriot* systems are useless against $500 plastic devices. It's a reversal of the cost of war: the insurgent spends $500 to destroy a $5 million asset.

3. Operation "Open Valve": Hydraulic Warfare

The real war is being fought underground. The pipeline network stretches for 15,000 kilometers.

The alliance has given rise to industrial **"hot tapping."**

1. **The Technique:** The insurgent engineers weld a bypass onto the high-pressure pipeline.
2. **The Theft:** Kilometers of buried flexible pipes divert 10% of the flow to hidden barges.
3. **Illegal Refining:** Stolen oil is refined in small, artisanal factories (*Cocinas*). The diesel produced is resold on the black market... and often bought back by the VRA through shell companies to fuel American generators! The US military buys its own stolen fuel.

4. Contamination: The "Orinoco Cocktail"

Sometimes, sabotage aims to destroy pure value.

In May 2027, insurgent technicians inject organic chloride compounds into the pipeline leading to the Jose terminal. The crude oil is loaded onto a **Titan Energy supertanker** . It arrives in Texas.

When it enters the Baytown refinery, the chlorine transforms into hydrochloric acid, causing rapid corrosion. The plant shuts down for six weeks. Cost: $200 million.

The insurgency struck American soil without firing a single missile. Insurers' confidence is collapsing.

5. The Intelligence Grey Area

The CIA and the NSA are blind.

- **SIGINT Failure:** The insurgents have reverted to analog (motorcycle messengers). The NSA cannot hack a whispered conversation.
- **The Betrayal of the Interpreters:** The local "fixers" employed by the US Army are often in the gang's pocket. Every American raid is leaked an hour in advance.

The American forces live in a bubble. In Maturín, the US Army thought it had pacified a neighborhood by building a school. In reality, as soon as night fell, the school served as an arms depot for the *Tren de Aragua* .

6. "April 19th": The Day the Lights Went Out

The coordinated offensive is launched on April 19, 2027 (the anniversary of independence). Operation **"Sovereign Darkness"** .

1. **Blackout:** Cyberattack on the power grid and destruction of pylons. Caracas is in the dark.
2. **Ambush: A Burton & Hall** logistics convoy is trapped in a tunnel. $50 million worth of equipment destroyed.

3. **Maritime attack:** Divers attach mines to two tankers at the José terminal. The ships are damaged, blocking the port.

On the morning of April 20, oil production fell by 40%. The "spread" (risk) on Venezuelan oil exploded on Wall Street.

7. The Salvadoran Option: "Colombianization"

Faced with the disaster, Washington activated the **Salvadoran Option** : outsourcing the dirty war to Colombian paramilitaries.

"Specialized contractors," veterans of the Colombian militias, were deployed by a front company funded by the CIA.

Their mission: to clear the jungle around the pipelines. They have no rules of engagement.

The Scorched Earth Strategy:

Starting in June 2027, the "Special Units" emptied the villages. 150,000 peasants were forcibly displaced. Those who remained were slaughtered. The Orinoco Belt became a human wasteland. Sabotage diminished, but hatred became absolute.

8. The Insurers' Nightmare (The London Syndicate)

The London Syndicate 's war risk committee classifies Venezuela as an **"Extreme Risk Area"** .

Marine insurance premiums increase from 0.1% to 5%.

Some reinsurers, like **Zurich Re,** refuse to cover land-based infrastructure.

Titan Energy and **AmeriCorp** must self-insure, tying up billions of dollars in capital. Venezuelan oil costs virtually **$65 a barrel** to produce (technical cost + security + corruption + insurance). It is no longer competitive.

9. The Moral Fracture and the "LeakSource" Scandal

On July 14, 2027, a US Army patrol stopped a truck driven by a Colombian mercenary transporting the bodies of tortured civilians.

The CIA intervened, freed the mercenary, and confiscated the evidence.

But the photos leaked on **LeakSource** and made the front page of the **New York Chronicle** .

The headline: **"In Venezuela, America funds its own butchers** . "

American public opinion shifted. 65% of Americans wanted the withdrawal.

10. The Aruba Deal: The Silent Surrender

September 2027. With the elections a year away, the American President cannot afford a stalemate. He decides to negotiate with the insurgency.

A secret meeting takes place in Aruba.

The "Deal" :

US emissaries propose a deal to the *MUC* :

1. **Amnesty:** End of the hunt for the leaders of the *Tren de Aragua* .
2. **Rent Sharing:** Integration of "local" security companies (controlled by the insurgency) into official oil contracts.
3. **Counterpart:** Cessation of attacks on pipelines.

America agrees to pay a revolutionary tax to its enemies to continue pumping. The agreement is signed. The attacks cease in October. Washington proclaims victory ("Pacification successful!"), but in reality, the US is paying rent to the warlords.

11. The Emergence of the "Narco-Petro-State" Under Tutelage

By the end of 2027, Venezuela had become a **Corporate Feudal Federation** .

- **Oil Enclaves:** Ultra-secure US coastal areas.
- **Middle-earth:** Transit zones run by gangs and paramilitaries, paid by **AmeriCorp** .
- **The Rest:** A lawless zone.

Drug trafficking has resumed, using the oil supply routes. The CIA turns a blind eye to preserve energy flows.

A. Petare's Bunker: The Shadow Command Center

Petare neighborhood, Caracas. April 10, 2027.

Petare is the largest slum in Latin America. A red brick labyrinth clinging to the mountainside, impenetrable to American *Stryker tanks* . In the basement of a butcher shop, in a disused cold storage room soundproofed with egg cartons, the

MUC (Mesa de Unidad Combatiente) war council was held .

Three men were looking at a holographic map of Caracas projected by a device stolen from **Flux Engineering** .

1. **General "El Maestro":** 60 years old, former strategist at the military academy. He wore an impeccable uniform, even when in hiding.
2. **The Prane "Killer":** 30 years old, leader of the *Tren de Aragua* . Tattoos up to his neck, gold teeth, playing with a butterfly knife.
3. **Engineer Santiago:** 45 years old, former head of SCADA systems at **PetroVen** . He looked like a math teacher, but he was the most dangerous man in the room.

Patriot air defense system is installed here at La Carlota Air Force Base," the General said, pointing to the map. "It covers all the airspace above 500 meters."

"We don't care about the 500 meters," Prane interrupted. "My kids fly at rooftop level." "The problem isn't the flying," said Engineer Santiago. "It's the jamming. **Sentinel Global** has installed frequency jammers around the electrical substations. If you get close to a standard drone, it drops like a fly."

Santiago placed an electronic chip on the table.

"That's why we're not going to use radio. We're going to use optics. I've reprogrammed the agricultural drones with image recognition software. We show them a picture of the electrical transformer. The drone searches for it, finds it, and flies straight at it. No pilot, no signal to jam. It's a poor man's smart missile." The General smiled.

— How many do you have ready?

— Five hundred.

— Good. Operation "April 19th" will be historic. We're going to turn off the lights in the Gringos' homes.

Prane stood up.

"And while they're in the dark, my men will handle the ground logistics. We're going to turn the Eastern Highway into a graveyard for **Burton & Hall trucks** ."

This alliance was unnatural. The soldier despised the gangster, the gangster mocked the engineer. But they had a common goal: to make the country ungovernable to force the occupier to pay the rent.

B. The Night of the Swarms: The "Pearl Harbor" of Drones

"El Sitio" electrical substation, Miranda State. April 19, 2027. 6:02 PM.

Florida National Guard Sergeant Johnson was bored. His mission: to monitor a high-voltage transformer in the middle of nowhere.

He was watching a video on his phone using the base's Wi-Fi.

"Hey, Sarge!" shouted Private Martinez. "Do you hear that?"

A buzzing. Like thousands of angry wasps.

Johnson adjusted his night-vision goggles. "Shit... What is that?" On the horizon, a dark cloud detached itself from the twilight sky. It wasn't airplanes. It was a wave.

— ALERT! DRONES! Fire!

The American soldiers opened fire with their M4s and heavy machine guns. Tracer bullets tore through the sky. They brought down ten, twenty.

But there were two hundred. The drones weren't trying to kill the soldiers. They ignored them. They dove down on the ceramic insulators and oil tanks of the transformers.

BOOM. BOOM. BOOM.

The explosions followed one another like firecrackers on a chain.

The boiling oil from the transformers ignited, creating a column of fire 50 meters high.

Then, silence. And blackness.

On the horizon, the lights of Caracas flickered and went out. Johnson looked at his phone. No signal.

"They tricked us," he murmured. "They tricked us with toys."

At the same time, 300 kilometers away at the Jose terminal, combat divers were attaching magnetic mines to the hull of the *AmeriCorp Freedom tanker* .

The attack was total. In one hour, the energy infrastructure that the US had spent a year "securing" was brought to its knees.

C. The Dirty Retaliation: The Arrival of El Carnicero

Hacienda "La Paz", State of Monagas. May 15, 2027.

The American response was swift. But it was not official.

In this isolated hacienda, transformed into a clandestine operations center, a CIA officer (code name "Bishop") was welcoming his new subcontractor.

The man who stepped out of the helicopter wore no insignia. He was short, stocky, with a neatly trimmed mustache. His name was **Jairo** , but everyone called him **"El Carnicero"** (The Butcher). He was a former commander of the *United Self-Defense Forces of Colombia* (AUC).

"Señor Bishop," Jairo said. "Your Marines are too soft. They follow the rules. Here, it's the jungle. The jungle doesn't follow the rules."
"That's why you're here, Jairo," Bishop replied, handing him a folder. "This is the pipeline map. We have constant attacks in these three sectors. The surrounding villages serve as a refuge for the saboteurs."
"You want me to arrest the saboteurs?"

— I want the attacks to stop. I don't want to know how. I just want the oil to flow. Your budget is $2 million a month, payable in cash or weapons, through our shell company **Sentinel Global** .

Jairo looked at the map. He smiled coldly.

"If we take away the water, the fish will die. We'll empty the villages. It will be..."

"Operation Cleanup".

— No cameras, Jairo. No witnesses. — With me, there are never any witnesses.

D. The Massacre of Santa Inés: Horror Seen from Above

Village of Santa Inés, near the Anaco-Jose Pipeline. June 2, 2027.

Corporal Rodriguez, a US Army drone operator based 50 km away, stared at his black and white screen. He was supposed to be providing "perimeter surveillance" for an allied operation.

What he saw made him vomit.

On the thermal imaging screen, figures were entering the village of Santa Inés.

They weren't American soldiers. They were El Carnicero's men. They weren't looking for weapons. They were dragging people out of their houses. Rodriguez saw the villagers lined up against the church wall. Men, women, children. He saw the thermal flashes of automatic gunfire.

The bodies collapsed like rag dolls.

Then, the men set fire to the houses with flamethrowers.

"Commander, this is Rodriguez!" he yelled into his microphone. "I see a mass execution! Sector 4! We must intervene!"

The voice of the duty officer in his headset was icy.

"Negative, Corporal. This is a partner forces operation. It's a free engagement zone."

— But they're killing civilians! I see children!

— Cut your video feed, Corporal. That's an order. Delete the recording. — But...

— CUT. It's classified "Omega". You didn't see anything.

Rodriguez turned off his screen. His hands were trembling. He had just realized that his uniform no longer represented the "Good Guys." He was the blind witness to a war crime.

E. The Escape: The USB Key of Truth

Bagram Air Base (nickname given to the Barcelona base), Venezuela. July 10, 2027.

Lieutenant Markus Wolf, Rodriguez's section leader, couldn't take it anymore.

He had seen the reports. He had seen the charred bodies when his patrols passed after the Colombians.

He had tried to speak to the Inspector General. He was told to keep quiet if he wanted his promotion.

That evening, Wolf entered the server room. He had the access badge.

He inserted an encrypted USB key. He downloaded everything.

Drone footage of the massacres.

The payment contracts between the CIA and the paramilitary front companies. The **Titan Energy memos** requesting a "final solution" for the troublesome villages.

He left the base. He went to a civilian internet cafe in Puerto La Cruz. He used the Tor network.

He sent the file, 12 gigabytes of evidence, to a single address:

contact@leaksource.org [1](WikiLeaks).

Then he threw the USB key down the drain.

He knew his career was over. Maybe his life. But he couldn't sleep with the blood of Santa Inés on his hands.

Three days later, the world awoke to the headlines in the **New York Chronicle** and the **Guardian** . The scandal was global. The image of

1. https://www.google.com/url?sa=E&q=mailto%3Acontact%40leaksource.org

"liberating" America was dead. It was replaced by the image of mass graves.

F. The Aruba Deal: The Surrender of the Superpower

Ritz-Carlton Hotel, Aruba. September 15, 2027.

After the scandal, the US Congress threatened to cut funding. Public opinion was outraged. The army was demoralized.

There was only one option left: to stop the war. Not by winning, but by paying.

In a presidential suite overlooking the turquoise sea, the CIA's Deputy Director, a weary man named Harper, faced his enemies.

Opposite him: a representative of the *Aragua Railway* in an Armani suit, and General "El Maestro" of the insurgency.

"We want the attacks to stop," Harper said. "The President wants the oil flowing for the election. That's all that matters."

"The oil will flow," said the General. "But on our terms."

— Which ones?

— 1. We want total amnesty.

— 2. Pipeline security contracts are transferred from your Colombian mercenaries to our own companies. We will protect the pipes ourselves... against ourselves. — 3. A tax of $5 per barrel is paid into an offshore account for "Social Development".

Harper did the math in his head. $5 per barrel, on 1.5 million barrels per day... that was $7.5 million per day. $2.7 billion per year.

America was going to fund the insurrection to stop it from firing. That was the very definition of racketeering.

"And if we refuse?" asked Harper.

The gang representative smiled.

— So we blow up José's terminal for good. And the price of gas in the US goes up to $10. You lose the election.

Harper sighed. He had no choice.

— Okay. But what do we call it in the press release? "Peace Agreements"? "National Reconciliation"?

— Call it what you want, Gringo. As long as the transfer arrives on the 1st of the month.

Harper signed.

At that moment, the United States ceased to be an occupying power and became a mere tenant paying rent to the local mafia. The war was over. Business resumed. But honor remained in Santa Inés.

Conclusion

The hybrid insurgency was not defeated militarily; it was integrated economically.

Oil flows to Texas, saving face. But the moral and financial cost is exorbitant. Venezuela is socially devastated.

This precarious stability rests on silence and accounting fraud. Oil companies conceal the true costs of this "security" in opaque balance sheet entries.

Now, a man on Wall Street is about to break this silence. The final collapse will not come from the jungle, but from the stock market.

CHAPTER 8: THE TRUTH CRASH AND THE NEW ENERGY ORDER

The "Subprime Oil" bubble, the liquidation of imperial dreams and the return of realism.

Lower Manhattan, New York. October 12, 2027.

Arthur Vance has never set foot in Venezuela. He can't tell the difference between an *arepa* and an *empanada* . Arthur Vance is a quantitative analyst for **Hades Capital** , a hedge fund specializing in short selling. His office is an air-conditioned glass fortress; his weapons are algorithms and balance sheets.

For the past six months, Vance has observed a statistical anomaly. Officially, everything is fine. The White House insists that Venezuelan production is a success. Shares of giants **Titan Energy** and **AmeriCorp** are at record highs.

But Vance's figures don't add up. By cross-referencing satellite data from tankers with customs declarations, he discovered a black hole.

- The volume of oil sold is inconsistent with the declared costs.
- Operational costs (OPEX) in Venezuela are abnormally low, given the ongoing civil war.

This morning, October 12, Vance published a research note entitled: **"THE CARACAS PONZI: Why Venezuelan Oil is the New Subprime"** .

In ten minutes, this document will do more damage to the American administration than all the brigades of the *Aragua Tren* combined.

1. The Anatomy of Fraud: The "Miracle" on Credit

The Vance report exposes the cover-up mechanism used to maintain the illusion of profitability.

For a barrel of Venezuelan oil to be profitable, it must cost less than $60 to produce. However, with security costs (**Praetorian mercenaries**), bribes to gangs (the "Tren Tax"), and marine insurance premiums from **The London Syndicate** , the real cost is **$85** .

How were **Titan Energy** and **AmeriCorp** able to post profits?

The Secret: Capitalizing on Losses.

The companies didn't record the additional security costs as **Current Expenses** (losses), but as **Capital Expenditure Expenses** (CAPEX), repayable over 30 years by the Venezuelan state.

It was pure fiction. Venezuela could never repay. The balance sheets were filled with toxic assets (phantom debts). It was a Ponzi scheme propped up by the implicit guarantee of Uncle Sam.

2. Black Tuesday for Energy

The market reaction is swift and decisive. Trading algorithms are reading the report.

At 9:30 a.m., at the opening of Wall Street:

- **AmeriCorp** stock falls by 12%.
- **Burton & Hall** shares plummeted by 18%.
- The "Venezuela Reconstruction" bonds, issued by the VRA, are reduced from 98 cents to 40 cents.

American pension funds, which had bought these "guaranteed" bonds, are seeing their portfolios collapse. This is no longer a geopolitical crisis, it's a domestic financial crisis.

3. Panic in the White House: The "Bailout" Dilemma

2:00 PM. Oval Office.

The Secretary of the Treasury delivers the bad news to the President:

"Mr. President, through the 'V-Account' mechanism at the Fed, we have technically guaranteed the liquidity of the system. If Venezuela does not pay the oil companies, it is the Federal Reserve that must pay."

The exhibition is worth **$150 billion** .

The President chooses the worst possible option: a temporary lie. He orders the Fed to quietly buy up the junk bonds. It's a massive money-printing operation to cover up a military blunder. Inflation surges again.

4. The Domino Effect: The End of the Petrodollar

In Riyadh, Saudi Arabia is watching.

"The Americans are cheating. They're printing dollars to subsidize their Venezuelan conquest. That dollar is now worthless."

On October 20, 2027, Saudi Arabia announced the end of the **peg** (fixed exchange rate) between the Riyal and the Dollar. From then on, Saudi oil would be sold in a basket of currencies including the Yuan.

The dollar falls by 15%. The price of imports to the US skyrockets. Gasoline at the pump exceeds $6 a gallon. Operation *Absolute Resolve* has destroyed American imperial privilege.

5. On the Ground: The Great Debacle (The Walk Away)

In Venezuela, as soon as funding stops (banks like **Manhattan Chase** cut off credit), the machine grinds to a halt.

On November 1, 2027, we witness the **"Walk Away"** .

- The unpaid mercenaries of **Sentinel Global** and **Praetorian are abandoning their posts.**
- The American engineers are being evacuated by charter flights.

Within 48 hours, the gangs and insurgents regained control of the terminals without firing a shot. America didn't leave because it had lost militarily. It left because the Excel spreadsheet had said "STOP."

In leaving, **Titan Energy** and **AmeriCorp** left behind an ecological disaster: overflowing toxic pits, open floodgates. Venezuela regained sovereignty over a toxic wasteland.

6. The "Red Vultures": The Cleaner's Strategy

Humboldt Hotel, Caracas. January 15, 2028.

Fog envelops the summit. A new signing ceremony takes place.

The signatories are the president of **SinoOil** (China) and General "El Padrino", head of the national reconciliation junta.

The document is a **Distressed Asset Management Agreement** .

China buys back the exploitation rights abandoned by the Americans for a symbolic dollar, in exchange for the cancellation of the debt.

By December, an airlift was in place. **China Petro engineers** arrived.

They replaced the sophisticated American digital systems with robust analog systems and **H-Tech** (Huawei) controllers. It's less efficient, but virtually indestructible.

In six months, production climbed back up to 1.5 million barrels per day. All the oil went to China. Venezuela became Asia's sole gas station.

7. The New Social Contract: "Pranocracy"

Within the country, a new political model is emerging: the **"Federal Pranocracy"** .

- **The Army** controls the borders.
- **The Gangs (Pranes)** govern the regions, collect taxes and provide policing.
- **The technocrats** manage the rent-seeking with the Chinese.

It's a violent but stable system. There's no more sabotage, because the gangs take a cut. Venezuela is pacified by the mafia, under Chinese tutelage.

8. Washington: Electoral Punishment and Retreat

In the US, the November 2028 election is being decided on the theme: "**Never again** . "

A new isolationist political force wins with the slogan "**Fortress America** . "

The new President implements a radical break:

1. **Complete withdrawal:** End of the Monroe Doctrine.
2. **Protectionism:** Ban on American oil exports. Texas must serve America first. Europe is abandoned.
3. **Debt cancellation:** The Treasury refuses to fully repay reconstruction bonds. Wall Street pays for its mistakes.

9. Epilogue: The Silence of the Orinoco

Faja del Orinoco, Junín Sector. February 2028.

Toyo Motors pickup truck rolls along a dusty track. Inside are a Chinese engineer and a Venezuelan foreman.

They pass the rusted skeletons of **Titan Machinery** (Caterpillar) machines abandoned by the Americans.

brand new **SinoOil** pumping station hums.

The Venezuelan points to the American ruins and laughs:

- *"They wanted to teach us how to work, but they didn't know how to survive here. They thought the oil belonged to whoever had the best drilling rig."*

The Chinese man stubs out his cigarette and replies:

- *"Oil belongs to no one. It belongs to the earth. We're just passing through to drink it. The Americans were in too much of a hurry. They choked."*

They arrive at the well. The Venezuelan opens the valve. The heavy crude begins to flow toward the sea, toward the supertankers waiting to depart for Beijing.

In the distance, salsa music can be heard coming from a village run by the *Aragua Railway* .

Life has resumed. It's not liberal democracy. But it's life as it is, sovereign, brutal, and resilient.

The Empire has withdrawn. The oil is flowing. And history continues.

END

www.ingramcontent.com/pod-product-compliance
Lightning Source LLC
LaVergne TN
LVHW022105200926
848481LV00003B/1063
9798233720246